In Search
of
Oneness

~~

Every Story Matters
And Needs to be Heard

I give you mine

~~~

Annette Erickson

Believe in you
& who you are
Trust the process.

Annette Erickson

Published by Annette Erickson
Email: annette@innerpathways.ca
Web: www.innerpathways.ca

In Search of *Oneness* – A Memoir of Hope and Healing
Annette Erickson
Copyright © 2015 by Annette Erickson

I have tried to recreate events, locales and conversations from my memories of them. In order to maintain their anonymity in some instances I may have changed the names of individuals and places, and I may have changed some identifying characteristics and details such as physical properties, occupations and places of residence.

Paperback:
ISBN-13: 978-0-9939887-0-7
ISBN-10: 0993988709

First published (eBook): January 27, 2015
ISBN: 978-0-9939887-1-4

Cover artwork and design by Digital Donna

I was born questioning
Not with words but within my heart and soul
An inquisitive but sensitive child
Wandering through the forest of humanity
Looking, feeling, touching, smelling
With the innocence of a child

Annette

Hold the Vision
Hear the Voice
Trust the Outcome

Mark David Gerson

Contents

PART TWO

Prelude

"**W**e have to be willing to go naked." This is what American poet and memoirist May Sarton said. These words are my willingness to go naked, to go beyond the doors of silence and secrecy, to push past the voices of my psyche, which started in infancy with, *"Hush little baby, don't say a word....*

From the time I was three years old, something in my heart pulled me to listen, and to pay attention, to look beyond what was visible. I didn't have the words to name, or the understanding to comprehend, much less know what to do with what I felt and knew inside. As I moved forward in life, this pull for the bigger picture grew into an insatiable hunger—a drawing force, a need to find my voice, a need for truth, connection and *Oneness* with myself, and the outside world.

This deep need to live a life of connection and *Oneness* consumed me, pulled me, but also frightened me. Yet a life not lived in truth, I soon realized, was a life not worth living. I needed to reach far down inside, as deep as I could go, connect with the passion that had always lived there, and find the words I had swallowed a long, long, time ago. Truth and voice would lead me to connection and *Oneness*. I was sure of it.

There's a saying, "Walk your talk." This is what I believe living my truth is about. It's about listening to the little, yet powerful voice inside me that is always there to guide me down the right path if I'm willing to listen.

For me, that little voice always refused to be silenced on the inside but I could never find the words to make that voice heard on the outside. The outside me had nothing to say. The inside me was like a volcano. I had plenty to say, but no voice to say it with.

The occasional word here and there never came close to saying everything I felt, or adequately conveyed the intensity of what I felt. I felt deeply and I tried to bury the intensity of it all for fear of scaring those around me. How could the adults in my life, especially those who were scared to feel, possibly understand my need for truth, connection and *Oneness*? How could they hear a child's voice—my voice, my words?

So, I discovered how to embrace the silence. And, often within the silence, I heard a voice like that of a young child pulling on my pant leg demanding me to pay attention, urging me to stop for a minute, bend down, and hear what she had to say. To listen to her words as she tried to guide me, "Listen. Listen. It's okay to feel the way you do. It's okay to feel and it's okay to be real."

The biggest challenge I've had to face on this journey is to identify and break down a limiting belief I adopted from the time I could walk—the belief that my words weren't important. This belief severed my voice and defined my experience like Picasso being forced to color inside the lines. It distanced me from the very thing I craved real, meaningful, deep, and intimate relationships. Unless I found a way to dismantle and rid myself of this belief, it would keep haunting me like the phantom pain from a severed limb.

This is my journey to find the words I couldn't speak, to live my truth and to live inside a circle of *Oneness* free of this phantom pain.

My hope is, not only that you might recognize yourself in the individual and the universal feelings and experiences that I had, but that through my words, you might touch the truth and the essence of who you are. Perhaps through my words, you too will come to a place where you can find your voice, own your story, and live a sense of *Oneness* with yourself, and the world around you.

I am reminded of the statue of the three monkeys sitting side by side. The first with his hands on his eyes: "See no evil," the second with his hands over his ears, "Hear no evil," and the third with his hands over his mouth, "Speak no evil." I always felt there should have been a fourth one with a hand over his heart, "Don't feel."

Even now, I clasp my hands over my ears as I strain to speak above the echo that warns me not to draw attention or bring shame to myself or to others. In my journey to touch truth, and to be real, I see, I hear, I write, I speak, and, yes, I feel. I have a voice and I am claiming the words that are mine to speak because I want to live with a sense of connection and *Oneness*, not only with myself, but also with you.

My journey into *Oneness* lies within a few basic, simple, wise words—"The truth shall set you free." These simple, yet profound words have burrowed under my skin. They form the basis of my travels. They are the North Star that shows me how to come home to the truth of who I am. Within truth lies the answer to the questions. Within truth is the embodiment of connection and *Oneness* I seek.

Through the many years I've worked as a counsellor, and the many times I've sat in both the client and the therapist chair, I've come to recognize within myself and others a deep inner hunger, a driving force within each of us, to live this sense of *Oneness*. This is my story.

PART ONE

Chapter 1

The Vision

Vision anchors and allows hope to seep through so courage can begin.

Something is not right. I don't know what it is and I don't know how I know. I just know. It's like when Dad forgets to take his hat off at church, or Mom leaves for town and forgets to put her lipstick on. I know it's not supposed to be that way, but I don't know why it's not supposed to be that way. I just know.

Something is just not there, and I don't have a word to describe what is missing. It's like when Mom said I had to eat my oatmeal when there wasn't any more brown sugar to put on it. How am I supposed to eat oatmeal with no brown sugar? Every spoonful makes my mouth water for what I know it can be, should be, and isn't. That's how I feel about things. My mouth waters for what can be, should be, and isn't.

The only time there is nothing missing and it feels right, is when everyone is sleeping. I sneak out of bed and make my way to the upstairs hallway window. The year is 1957. I am a child. I am five years old. It's at this window that it begins to happen.

The old-fashioned slider window divided into squares makes me think of the patchwork quilt on Grandma's bed. She told me once that every square patch in her quilt had a story behind it. When I look at the window, I know that behind each of those squares there's a story too.

It is the only window in the house that opens by sliding sideways, and the only one I can reach and open myself. Even on days when it is so cold outside that the school bus can't come for us, and the window refuses to budge, I still make my way to the window.

I like being at the window. It's easier to breathe. I like looking out where there's all this space. I can see lots. I can see everything or forever. I can see the big blue sky, the sun, the moon, or the stars. Unless they are all hiding behind the clouds. It reminds me that I hide stuff too. So, I watch to see what happens, and I see the clouds move back and forth, and watch as the sun, the stars, or the moon pop back up as if they never even went anywhere; as if they just had a shadow pass over them. Sometimes there are shadows that pass over me too.

I wonder if they get scared like me, and wonder what they would do if they couldn't find their way out from behind the clouds. I come to the window often, and the clouds always move, so I know they're not stuck like the stuff inside of me. That's why I like looking out the window. I get to be part of what I see, and what I know can be.

I see people. They are not people I know, but I'm not afraid of them. They are real. They speak, laugh, and smile. I can tell they like each other and they care, because they hug, and hold hands. They're not afraid to tell each other things, or to cry, or to touch each other in caring ways. When I watch them, I feel all warm inside like when I take a hot bath.

I know words are important for these people, because when someone talks, everyone listens. Not just a pretend listen, but a real listen, the kind of listening that happens even through the noise. Like when my cat, Tiger, hears the mouse that no one else hears. That's how these people listen. It feels right when people listen. It feels warm and safe.

That's why I keep coming to the window. It feels good—the same as when the sun pokes out from behind the cloud on a cool day, and irons the goose bumps out of my skin. Same-same.

When I stare out the window, it feels as if I am part of that world too. I can see it and I can feel it inside me. I know this kind of world is possible. I know I'm going to find it and live it one day.

I want that kind of world where people are all connected, like the cutout paper dolls my friend likes to make. When people are all connected, they want to understand what is being said, or not said, and it makes it easy to tell people stuff. There's no pretending in that kind of world. It's real.

In the kind of world I live in down here, I don't talk much, except when I'm by myself, or when I'm with my cat or my dog. They always want to listen. Besides, they have built-in radar. It makes them perk up their ears, listen, and pay attention to what's really going on around them, and lets them know if there's danger around the corner.

I watch how they stop dead in their tracks, and how every fibre of their body stands at attention just like when I rub a balloon on my head and my hair stands up by itself. They know when it's not safe, but they also know when people are having a grumpy day or feeling sad or scared. I'm a lot like my cat and my dog. I know too.

I'm just learning to read books now, but I've been able to read what people say with their bodies since forever. I can read their face and tell things by their mood or the way their voice sounds when they say things. Sometimes they say more when they're not saying anything at all, and sometimes that's even scarier.

So I can pretty well figure out what I can or can't talk about, what people will listen to, and what they won't, or can't. That's why I am like my cat and my dog. I have built-in radar too. Most of the time what I live, I keep to myself, especially when it comes to what I see, and how it feels in my heart. When I try to talk about any of that, people think I'm just a kid with a wild imagination.

I don't understand. What I see is much more than imagination, and I'm not playing pretend games. They are the ones that are playing games and pretending about all kinds of things. So why should I tell them what I see, feel, and know from sitting at my window, I keep that all well hidden so no one can make fun of it or brush it off like cat hair on their dress clothes. I've decided it's "my" secret, "my" vision, and I'll keep it that way.

I won't let grown-ups make fun of something I know for sure of how people can live in this world. I won't let them take that away from me. Just because they can't hold on to the magic, it doesn't mean that the magic isn't there or that the visions I see aren't real. They are so real!

So when everyone is asleep, I go to my window and let my thoughts wander and drift against the cold dark of the night, and it doesn't take long before I feel all warm and fuzzy inside. That's when I reach out to a place past a million stars and planets, a place in the unknown, where answers wait to be discovered.

The seeker is alive in me, always needing, wanting and believing there has to be more. As strong as the need to run in the face of danger is, the need to sit by my window and the promises it holds, urges me to return. When I show up at my window I feel connected to something bigger, and hope someday, somehow, this something will be revealed to me.

Images appear in my mind against the backdrop of a moon hanging in the far corner of a starlit sky. With Alberta Northern Lights dancing all around, I drift in this serendipitous world of images without words.

I see people mingling together. In some places there are two or three people gathered and in other places there are groups of four or five, but everywhere I look I see the same kind of look on people's faces. It must be the same kind of look I get on my face when I'm concentrating on reading new words or watching a butterfly crawl out of its cocoon. The way they look at each other and their undivided attention tells me nothing is more important to them than the moment they are in. And when I sneak in closer so I can hear what they're saying, I can tell people are free to express what they feel without stumbling over their words. Nobody feels embarrassed, silly or afraid to say what they feel. They speak from their heart and it just spills out of them as smoothly as syrup oozing from a maple tree. There is no shame. People don't hesitate in the expression of who they are. Love is okay. I am like the fish who bites on the lure. I am hooked!

Instead of a five-year-old dreaming about Santa Claus and Snow White and the Seven Dwarfs, I am drawn to a whole other world. A world I am eager to jump into like when I run outside to make my first snow angel of the year.

Just like when Mom pulls the drawstring beside our living room window and the curtains open to reveal the magic of the day, I stare into the vastness of the darkened sky and wait until the moon, the stars, or the different shades of light and dark reveal the magic of the night.

Tonight, in my vision, I see a group of eight people, both young and old sitting in a circle, and each one is encouraged to share something while others sit quietly and listen to what each person has to say. I join them. It feels safe within that circle. Soon it is my turn. I decide I can use my voice. I decide to speak.

"My heart is full," I tell them. "I feel things very deep inside me. When I am around others, I can feel what they are feeling even if they don't say or do anything. I connect with them. I feel their energy. I want to put my arms around them and let them know they are not alone, and I wish I could feel free to do that, but I'm afraid some people won't understand, or even want to listen to me because I'm only five years old. I'm scared they will think I'm crazy if I go sit beside them, and let them know it is okay to feel what they're feeling. Still that's what is in my heart, and I so much want to learn how to be true to what is in my heart."

I stop. Everyone is silent. The silence does not threaten. It is inviting me. I continue.

"I don't want to live in a world where people don't connect to each other, or where the words 'I love you' can't leave anyone's lips, even when they feel it in their heart. If a person feels love, why can't they say so? Why can't they say, "I love you?" Why do people play pretend games and never say what they really feel. Most of the time I can tell what they're feeling, and often it's not the same as what they're saying."

I take a deep breath then and tell the people, "That is all I have to say."

An older man with light tousled hair almost down to his shoulders, and eyes the color of the sea, looks directly at me and speaks next.

"This is a place of learning. You can come here anytime. You are welcome to take part, to sit and listen, to observe, to feel, to take it home with you. This is as it should be and it's all possible. Don't ever let anyone lead you to believe otherwise. Stay true to what you feel in your heart. This is what will let you connect with people and one day you will be able to live it in your world."

My eyes fill with water, like when my cat Tiger or my dog Tippy lick my face and love me when I feel sad. I look around and I know people have heard, and people have understood, and my heart feels like I've just had an early Christmas. I say thank-you, leave this group of people, and go see what else I can find.

There are other groups of two or more immersed in conversation, listening with their hearts, not just their ears. People are talking about who they are, what they love, think or feel, and no one feels embarrassed or threatened. There are no confused looks or looks of fear when they share words from their heart, or when they touch one another and live moments of intimacy. People give and receive. It all makes sense to me. It's like having brown sugar for my oatmeal. Things are as they should be. There is no fear, no judgment, and no doubt. There is acceptance, love, and sharing.

The vision tells me people can be real and can be true to who they are but first they have to be willing to let go of their pretend self and to reach in and grab their real self and to live from there. This is the world I see when I slide the window open and look out into the night—it's a world where if people say, they love you, it's because they mean it and if they touch you or do something for you, it's because they care and it comes from their heart, No one even thinks of lying or pretending because everyone is true and real. It's a world where there's meaning, love, laughter, and a sharing of what is, whether that be pain or joy or fear. This is the kind of world that wraps its fingers around my heart and that I so desperately want to live—a world where people are *One* with themselves, with each other, and the world they live in. I need to find a way to bring this world I see to me.

Hi...,
I'm sitting at my window.
I don't know what to call you...
A vision?
Are you real?
You should have a name you know?
I'll be back.
I hope you will, too.
Ti-Lou
(but you can call me Lou).

Chapter 2

The Name Game

Admitting to truth isn't always easy but necessary.

I not only grew up with two languages, I also grew up with two names.

That could have nothing to do with, or everything to do with, my struggle to be me and to feel one with the world around me.

I arrived into this world in mid-afternoon in a small northern Alberta town on a cool but sunny Easter weekend—an April day when the snow was slowly melting to reveal the frozen ground below.

It was 1952; a year when the Liberals were in full force with Louis St. Laurent as Prime Minister, and the headlines announced the Canadian surplus was at an all-time high of $390,400. A time when a loaf of bread cost twelve cents, a gallon of milk eighty-four cents and you could build a new home for $16,000.

On the day of my arrival, old "Doc Fiske," a down-to-earth, no-frills man who doesn't feel a need to hide behind big fancy words to prove who he is, or how much he knows, assists in my delivery into this world. He is a short, stubby guy who shuffles his feet when he walks, has half glasses that balance on the tip of his nose, fingers that are yellowed with nicotine from years of smoking, and the smell of booze and rubbing alcohol emanating from his pores.

From what I know, the name Ti-Lou (Little Wolf), or Lou for short, was bestowed upon me shortly after I appeared. Perhaps my first cries echoed through the hospital corridors like a wolf howling at Grandmother Moon shining high in the night sky. Or it could be that I arrived with a voice desperately needing to be heard, and a deep need for an inner connection that was already stirring me from the inside out.

The following year, my dad gets into trouble.

"What are your children's names?" the taxman asks my dad.

My father promptly replies with the names of my brother Richard, my two sisters Danielle and Lucie, then adds, "And the youngest one is Ti-Lou."

"Girl or boy?"

"Pardon me?"

"The youngest one, Ti-Lou, girl or boy?"

"A girl."

"Ti-Lou. Is that her real name? Is that the name on her birth certificate?"

Even before the taxman reaches the question mark, my dad knows he's in trouble. He quickly considers his options. Maybe he can do his little jig and dance, something that often comes in handy either to attract attention or to distract someone from something. It also serves him well to relieve tense moments.

How could he forget the name of his own child? He tucks his chin down and slides his fingers down the rim of his hat spinning it around in his hands. Once more, he scans his memory bank. Louise, Lucille, Louella? What else could it be? Lisa? No, that's not it either.

The taxman raises his eyebrows, looks over the top of his glasses and gives my father an, "Are you serious?" kind of look. Dad has no choice but to fess up.

"I don't remember," he says keeping his eyes downcast as he feels his cheeks get warm. "Since the day she was born we've always called her Ti-Lou, and I can't remember what her real name is now. It just won't come to me."

And that's about as much as I know about the story of how I got the name Ti-Lou—a name that has followed me throughout the years like gum stuck to my shoe. What I know more about is the journey I've been on, the journey to understand, reconcile and integrate the two: Annette and Ti-Lou.

For the first five years of my life, Ti-Lou, or Lou, is what I answer to. Then one day, a strange man is invited to our house for supper. When I walk into the kitchen where Mom and Dad are having coffee with him, they introduce him to me as the schoolteacher, Mr. Lebeau.

When he sees me, Mr. Lebeau stands. By the time his skinny frame has unfolded, he towers over Mom by a couple of heads, and it only takes him two steps to reach me clear across the room. Then he folds himself back up like an accordion, reaches for my hand and sandwiches it between his. His eyeballs the color of dirty water peer into mine. Something in my stomach twitches and makes me want to get away. I glance towards the door. That's when I hear Mom say, "Mr. Lebeau, this is our youngest daughter, Annette."

"Huh?"

I look behind me to see if someone else has entered the room. No one has. Besides my mom and dad, and this man, there's no one else in the room but me. I wait for Mom to take her words back and correct her mistake, but instead I hear her say, "We've always called her Ti-Lou, but her name is really Annette."

I pull my hand away so it will be closer to my own body where it belongs, and run over to Mom. Half-crying, half-shouting, I manage to blurt out, "That's not true. That's not my name!" And that's when I am assured that, yes indeed, it is my real name, and that it's the name I will have to use when I go to school. I try to protest, but they have already launched into a full-fledged discussion, and I can tell they aren't interested in hearing what I have to say.

Together they discuss how much I already know and how quickly I learn. I hear Mr. Lebeau say that even though I only turned five in April, he feels I will be ready to start grade one in September, which is only a couple of months away. Then the man, who is as tall as a Christmas tree looks at me again, and as if he knows what it's like for me, calmly says, "Don't you worry. It won't take long for you to get used to the name Annette." My mom nods and agrees.

I quickly scan their faces for something to tell me this is all a pretend game, but Mom and Mr. Lebeau are already busy flipping the pages on the calendar to check on the start date for my first day of school. I open my mouth to protest, but nothing comes out. My words are stuck inside.

"That name is not who I am. It doesn't feel like me. It isn't me. I don't want to be someone else. I want to be me. What's wrong with being Ti-Lou?"

My eyes dart over to Dad. Surely, he will help me. But he just looks at me and says, "See, you're a very lucky girl. Instead of having just one name you have two."

As I walk out the door, I keep saying to myself, *"I only have one! I only have one!"*

Dear...,
I need a name for you.
Do you want one of mine?
They tell me I have two.
Annette and Ti-Lou.
I don't like having two names.
I don't know which is true.
I don't know which is me.
Do you?
From me, (the one who wrote to you before).

Chapter 3

Dick & Jane

Truth, it feels so big, so overwhelming - at the same time it entices me to come forward and put pen to paper.

When it is time for reading practice, I am instructed to stand beside him, behind his massive wooden desk with two drawers on each side, and a smaller but wider one in the middle that can be locked with a key. Sometimes I stare at the keyhole and wonder if the drawer is actually locked, or if there is a way I can shrink myself, slide through the keyhole and hide out in the drawer where no one can find me.

If I stand close enough, I can rest my chin on top of the desk. There are initials carved into it that look like tattoos and ink and coffee stains that look like puzzles from my coloring book. The school teacher, Mr. Lebeau, the white-haired giant with a moustache the size of a paint brush and hands the size of baseball mitts, wraps his furry arm around me and pulls me close between his knees, then instructs me to read out loud.

"Go ahead," he says, after he's told the other twelve or fifteen kids from grades one to eight to keep their nose in their books and buckle down to their assigned work. And buckle down they do, even if there is no other teacher to watch over them and make them do their work. When he speaks, everyone listens, otherwise they know they'll be in trouble. Once the class settles, he turns to me.

"Start reading," he says. I immediately obey.

"Fun with Dick and Jane." I begin. "See Dick play. See Jane laugh. See Dick and Jane have fun and laugh."

"Good job," he whispers in my ear while his fingers make their way inside my clothes and he starts on what he refers to as one of his treasure hunts. "Good job!" he says aloud as he pulls me in even closer between his spread out legs. "Good job!"

"Look said Jane," I continue. "Look up. Look all the way up."

"Yes, that's it, keep reading. You're doing very well."

"Dick and Jane ran. Spot ran too. Run Spot run. Run all the way home!"

I want to run too, but there is nowhere to run. There is nowhere to hide. These are just stupid make-believe books. I can't run all the way home.

The school bus has dropped us off at a school out in the country on a piece of land miles away from home, with nothing in sight except for a little white house at the back of the school. This house, I soon discover, is the teacher's house. Sometimes, when all the other kids are busy playing, he takes my hand and takes me there, and gives me candy for being such a good girl and for doing such a good job of reading to him out of my Dick and Jane reader.

I don't remember much about his house except that it smells like the inside of my dad's work boots when he comes back from working in the field all day, and it has squeaky floors and tiny windows I can't see out of unless I climb on a chair. What I remember more is the one-room schoolhouse.

I remember the potbelly stove in the middle of the room, the leather strap in the back cupboard next to the hooks on the wall where everyone's coats are lined up like the little green army soldiers the boys play with. I remember my old school desk with the flip top where I store my reader, my scribbler, my two HB pencils, my pink gum eraser, my pencil sharpener, my 12 inch wooden ruler and my box of wax crayons.

I remember how I lift the top of my desk to steal a peek inside, and how good it feels to know that the way things are placed and look is totally up to me. I am in control of what happens in there. No one else but me.

I remember a map of the world that takes up most of the wall on the right side of the room. The wall on the left side has windows, and I can see the top half of the biggest most gigantic poplar tree in the schoolyard; the one I want to hide behind so no one can find me.

I don't remember where my two sisters sit, where we go to get the wood to stoke the fire in the potbelly stove, or where we wash our hands after we use the outhouse. I don't remember the exact sound of the leather strap when it hits the older boys' open hands when they misbehave. I only remember how deafening it is when it echoes and bounces off every surface in the room. I remember how it makes me cringe and shrink a notch deeper into my seat.

I don't remember at what time I am allowed to go get my tin lunch box from the shelf at the back of the room underneath the row of tiny soldier coats, or how much time I have to eat my peanut butter sandwich, apple and cookie mom put in my lunch box before I left for school.

I remember the report cards Mr. Lebeau gives me to bring home, and how very proud my parents are of me when my lowest mark is a whopping 97%. Scrawled in his handwriting there are comments like: "Annette is a very intelligent little girl and does very well in school. Annette is learning how to read and is doing good work in all her subjects." The hand who wrote those is the same hand that travels and explores my body for the first two years that I go to school.

Annette is the one who got those good marks. Not me.

I remember how the eight miles from home to that little one room schoolhouse seems like going to the other end of the world. I remember kids calling me *teacher's pet*, and how that starts a fire inside my belly that stays there all day. I see pictures travel through my mind like watching a movie. In the movie, I am big enough and strong enough to knock those kids down, spit in their faces, scratch their eyes out, and run into the wind as fast as my feet can carry me and never ever come back. Instead, I freeze, and the words I want to scream become lodged at the back of my throat like a logjam at the mouth of a river. My face turns as red as the maple leaf on the Canadian flag that beats in the wind, and like me, can't get free.

I don't remember other kids having to read at the teacher's desk, going to the teacher's house at recess, or being called teacher's pet, but that doesn't mean there wasn't any. There could have been. What I remember are the secrets that weigh me down like when I try to walk with my dad's big work boots that are ten times too big for me. I remember the tremors in my body, his warm hand on my cold skin, and how my body betrays me by not letting me run far away. I don't remember how I try to tell my mom what happens, but I remember I try to find words to describe things I have no words for, and how she doesn't understand what I say.

And I remember how she repeats to me that Mr. Lebeau is a kind, gentle man, and I have to be a good girl, and that there is nothing to be afraid of.

I don't remember how long it is between the day I try to talk to my mom and the day I burst into tears and say how much I hate school and don't want to go anymore. But I remember how Dad gets mad, and how he says, "Quit being such a cry baby. Get out there and get on that bus before it leaves without you." And I remember how I trip and fall when he shoves me towards the door, and a lump the size of my fist lodges itself in the back of my throat, and how the river of lava starts to flow inside me. I don't remember anything else about that day, except how I glare at my dad for a second before I get up, and in that moment, I decide snakes will grow wings before he ever sees me cry again.

Things I remember and things I don't remember are different from the things I know. I know I came from a place of wrongful initiation, an initiation that doesn't belong to a child, and I escaped by careful monitoring, examination and discernment. Like the blind whose ears and fingers become supersensitive to different sounds and touches, I become supersensitive to people's moods, feelings and energy flow. I make it my job to discern, calculate, and intuit with all my senses, and I learn to sharpen and master them like a pro.

Before I am even old enough to tie my own shoes or reach into the kitchen sink, I am introduced, initiated if you will, into an adult world I am not ready to enter. I am too little to have the right words to put experience into form, nor do I have the ability to gather and decipher the vast range of questions and emotions that prevail.

Am I special the way I'm being told I am? Am I different, bad, evil maybe? Is that why these things happen to me? Who am I supposed to listen to? Who will listen to me? Who will believe me? What can I say? What can I do? This is not the way it's supposed to be. I have to find answers to all my questions. I have to find ways to make things different.

I'm feeling one thing while my voice says the words I read on the page. Words I concentrate on getting right. Words that have nothing to do with what I'm feeling while fingers explore pieces of me I don't even know I have.

My own fingers shake as I turn the pages. I try not to miss any words, try not to show any expression on my face in case someone looks my way, and they know about the fingers travelling between my legs. No one can find out, or they will tease me and make fun of me. I am on high alert, hyper-vigilant to the nuances of each moment.

My insides tell me what is happening is wrong, but I don't know how to right it. I want to scream, but screaming is not allowed. I want to run, but there is nowhere to run? Read. That's what I need to do. I have to read. I have to finish the page and get it right. If I don't make any mistakes, I will finish quicker, he will have to let me go sit down, and then I can check inside my desk to make sure things are still in the same order I placed them, and then everything will be alright.

People tease me about being little by saying things like a gust of prairie wind will blow me clear across the countryside, but that's okay. People won't be able to make fun of me and tease me about what the teacher does to me. Besides, I love the feel of the wind on my face, and when the peacefulness of the night brings me to my favorite window, I don't feel little. I don't feel like a child.

I sit in the quiet of the night and press my face against the window. It doesn't take long before images appear and my heart soaks in what my mind can see. People are kind and don't make fun of others here. When people touch it's the kind of touch that doesn't hurt or make them squirm inside. Stories aren't make-believe like in that stupid Dick & Jane reader. Truth lives here. There are no lies and it leaves me feeling all warm and peaceful inside like when I snuggle with my blanket by the campfire and sip on a hot-chocolate.

The outside world is often so different than what the vision shows me, but I know what the vision shows me is possible and I know it's the way it's supposed to be. I just know it. I have to find a way to hang on to that vision and bring it home to me.

Dear ...,

I still don't have a name for you.

Annette is not the right name for me. Not the real me.

She's the one who reads and gets good marks at school, but I don't even know if those marks are true.

The books the teacher makes me read aren't true. They are just make-believe. So maybe the marks he gives me aren't true either. Maybe they're just make-believe too.

Why can't I just be Ti-Lou?

I have two names and you don't even have one. I really need to find a name for you but it has to be the "right one."

That's it! Now I know what to call you!

I'll be back in a minute. Mom is calling me.

~~~

Dear One:

What do you think of the name? I think it's perfect. After all, you're "the One" who's always there.

Can I call you One?

You listen to me. You believe me. You don't lie to me. I like that about you.

Will you help me find out what is true?

I don't like to pretend and I don't like people who pretend.

You feel real and I like talking to you. Can you help me be real too?

I hope you like your name.

Mine is Ti-Lou. Lou for short.

Chapter 4

On My Own

Truth doesn't mean that we never make a mistake or tell a lie; it means we continually realign ourselves to what is true for us.

We live on a farm seven miles from a hamlet of about three hundred people to the southeast of us, and a town of about one thousand people eight miles to the southwest. When we are in need of a dentist, school clothes, shoes, or a brand new batch of yellow chicks to keep us supplied with fresh eggs, we go to a bigger center called Peace River, which is about forty-five miles to the North.

Where we live on the farm, people say you can watch your dog run away from home for three days and still see which direction he is headed, but when we go to Peace River, it is different. It's like dropping into a magical place and regardless of the season it feels like candy to my eyes. It never ceases to mesmerize me.

The trees, the river that winds its way through the bottom of the valley, the hills, as far as I can tell, uninhabited and unexplored by man—all the beauty that stretches before my eyes awakens within me the same kind of warmth and connection I feel at night when the visions come to me. Each time we make our way down the hill to the town center, I plaster my face to the car window, stare into the hills and feel a pull for what I feel can be and should be within all of us all the time—a feeling that arms are wrapped around us and holding us close—a feeling that we are all the same—that we are connected to everyone and everything. I so much need to talk about all this, but how do I talk about something that can't be seen, something I have no name for, and no words to describe.

I go to a different school now. When I was in the middle of grade two, the one room schoolhouse closed and Mr. Lebeau disappeared. I wonder. Did he disappear because of me?

When I am at home, I often go play pretend games in a patch of evergreen trees about half a mile away from our house. I pretend I am in charge of all the animals in the forest and my job is to protect them and keep them safe. Other times I sit under a tree, reading *Huckleberry Finn* or the *Adventures of Tom Sawyer* and enjoy how this time it's the crows, robins, chickadees, squirrels, rabbits and other critters, who are there to protect and watch over me.

When I am old enough to be trusted with the .22 rifle, I squat in the tall grass by our dugout at the edge of my little forest and wait patiently for the occasional muskrat that finds its way into our drinking water and mucks it up. I've been warned many times that if I get one not to try to pull it out of the water or I might fall in. I've never said, but they don't have to worry much. I always aim to miss cause I don't like killing things.

I am teetering between two worlds. One day I'm content with skipping rope, twirling a baton, or sitting by myself by the dugout shooting a .22, and the next day I'm bike riding and developing a friendship with a childhood sweetheart Jacques and his friend Marcel.

My other companions are the many cats and dogs that make their way in and out of my life. They are my friends, my playmates and my confidants. They are the holders of my troubles, and my dreams.

Once in a while, I stay with a friend who lives in town and we get to go to the Saturday matinee. After watching an action packed Tarzan or John Wayne movie, we often pretend to be them. I enter their world and become the cowboy who rides my horse and roams across the land in search of the bad guy, settles into my sleeping bag by a campfire, and watches the moon make its way across the sky. Another day I am Tarzan swinging from the vines about to save someone or something from impending doom.

Going to stay in town for the weekend is fun, but life on the farm is way better. I like living where I can hear the frogs croak at night, smell the green pasture, watch our garden grow from seeds to plants we water, and watch our land transform from a field of dirt to a field of wheat that towers high above my head, and shimmers like gold in the afternoon sun. We often work from sun-up to sun-down, but at the end of the day we slide our hands together and it looks like we're brushing crumbs off of them, but what we're saying is the job is done, and it's time to grab a book or the fishing tackle and rod. Or, sometimes we just jump in the car and go for a drive to go explore or visit friends, neighbours and relatives.

Then there is that one weekend when I am around six years old when something in me shifts, and from that moment on, I start to live life differently. Although not all that significant when looking at it from the outside, what happens changes something inside of me that stays with me like initials carved in a tree. For Mom and Dad, like for many other adults, socializing and unwinding from all the hard work also means having a few drinks. On this one particular weekend, Mom, Dad and me load up the truck and make our way to Winagami Lake Provincial Park where many of their friends are joining us for a picnic.

Today there are four couples and there are more bottles of every color size and shape decorating the table than I've ever seen before but everyone is happy and having a good time. I am free to go make castles in the sand, play on the swings, merry-go-round, and in the water, as long as I stay close to shore and do regular check-ins with them.

When the sun starts to set over the lake and the air starts to cool, I decide to make my way back to camp and go warm up by the fire. As I approach the spot where we set up camp, it sounds like there are twice as many people as before but when I get there I don't notice anybody new, it's just that everyone looks and sounds different somehow. Their voices are loud and their words are slurred like they just come out of a dentist office and they are doing and saying silly things like teasing or poking each other around.

The men and women are talking at the same time and talking over each other. They laugh at anything and everything and a lot of what they say doesn't even make sense. Every now and then they break into uncontrollable laughter or a chorus of off key voices singing, "Ahh...du bon vin j'en ai bu."

A sick kind of feeling forms in the pit of my stomach; the kind I get when I find myself in water over my head and I don't have anything to hang on to. I start darting around looking for my mom, and when I finally spot her, my breath gets stuck in my rib cage and can't find a way out. The queasy feeling in the pit of my stomach grows and my body starts to shake. What I've found is not her but a shadow of her.

Something has taken her away and I know what it is. I've seen it before. It's the same thing that often snatches my dad away. The drinks make the real him disappear, only to return sometime later in the evening, the next day or sometimes not until two or three days later. I hate and fear those days, but I always have my mom to run to, feel safe with, and rely on. But not this time.

This time she too, has gone to wherever it is people go when they drink too much; a world I cannot understand, comprehend or in any way wish to be part of. A world far from my window.

The party is coming to an end and everyone is packing up.

"Will you be okay to get home?" ask a few of my parents' concerned friends.

"Sure. Sure. We will be fine," Dad says as he gets behind the wheel. I get in next to him and Mom sits on the passenger side.

Usually Mom is the one who gets behind the wheel after Dad has been drinking, but tonight she is worse than Dad. I want to tell them, "I'll do it. I'll get us home. I'll drive." But so far the only time I have been behind the wheel is when Dad has let me sit on his lap, and he did whatever needed to be done with the pedals while I turned the wheel, and it's been daylight out so I could see where I was going. With only headlights to guide me, how would I find our way home?

We haven't gone more than a few miles down the road when Mom yells. "Stop!" Dad slams on the brakes and the truck comes to an abrupt stop on the side of the road. Mom staggers her way out of the truck into the ditch where she heaves and heaves as her insides come spilling out like when Tiger puked on my bed. Dad orders me to stay in the truck and goes out to help her. He doesn't need to tell me to stay put. My own inner terror freezes me. I cannot move.

I sit in the truck. It feels big, empty, and cold. I watch Mom get sick in the ditch as Dad wobbles next to her, trying to help her somehow. Thoughts race through my mind... my real mom and dad are gone. I am defenseless, vulnerable, and naked. I'm lost. I want to be brave, but I don't know what to do to be brave. My thoughts scare me. Is Mom going to die? Will we all die? There's no one to ask. I am alone. So terribly alone. Mom and Dad are there. I see them, but they are not there. Not really. We are not connected. We are separate from one another. I am on my own.

It becomes as clear as the day I started school, I am not only alone—I am on my own. There is no one to go to, no one to talk to; I am trapped, have no voice, and no one I can tell what I feel inside.

Dear One:

I'm even more confused.

I don't only have two different names. I live in two different worlds.

One world feels so real and so true, but isn't really what I live in. The other world, the one I find myself in, can feel so unreal, so untrue and so empty sometimes. Not all the time, but sometimes.

That's when I feel lost, scared, lonely and alone. That's when I need to hold Tiger in my arms or be perched up high in the arms of a tree where I can feel my heart beat to the rhythm and the pulse of the One that supports me.

Ti-Lou

Chapter 5

Roots and Fears

Truth can define our lives as we blaze our own trail along unbeaten paths.

Five years old was a significant marker on my mom's time line as it was in mine.

She is the fourth child in a family of five children and she is five years old when her mother, my grandmother, becomes very ill, and is later hospitalized with depression and what they suspect is an infection resulting from bad teeth. They decide to administer an anesthetic to pull the teeth, but when she comes out of the anesthetic, she is no longer the same.

She doesn't recognize anyone, she doesn't speak, and she can't do anything for herself. The doctor tries everything he can think of to help her. When he no longer knows what else to do and she doesn't show any signs of improving, he suggests that she be admitted to a facility in Edmonton. My grandfather chooses to take her home instead.

My grandmother is in a semi-comatose state and instead of having a mother to look after her, my mom, along with her siblings, are the ones looking after their mother. They feed her, wash her, brush her hair, clip her nails, read to her, and everything else that is required for her care until their father and their two uncles come home from work on the land. They do this for the next seven years.

In my father's life, when he is fifteen years old, a fire rages through their home and he watches in horror as his mother, now safely out of the house, runs back in to try to save her fifteen-month-old twins and another one of her children. No one comes back out. After this, my grandfather drinks too much, frequents other women and is unable to be present to himself, never mind his children. The four younger ones are sent to live in a convent and my dad and his older brother decide to set out on their own to earn a living.

I wonder if perhaps, like me, both my parents gazed at the night sky in search of a sense of connection which they couldn't quite reach or wrap their heart around in their everyday world.

Dad works in forestry camps or for farmers until he has enough money to purchase his own homestead. Mom goes to work for neighbors helping them with their children, cooking, cleaning, and doing laundry. Then one day both of them meet at a dance held at a local hall. A short time later, in 1939, Dad proposes to Mom and they get married. He is 26. She is 17. Together they settle on the homestead where they grain farm as well as raise their own cows, pigs and chickens. Mom also plants huge gardens and cans her produce so they will have food to help them through the long, harsh northern prairie winter months.

I wonder if, like me, there are times when Mom and Dad live an inner connection with the deeper part of themselves. And I wonder if, like me, they feel a continuous rumble in their soul, a hunger to live this connection with everything and everyone in their outside world.

If someone needs a piece of iron welded, Dad tells him to bring it over. If the next door neighbor isn't finished his harvest, Dad offers to go help him complete before the rain comes. Even when total strangers run out of gas or slide off the icy roads, Dad wastes no time in bringing some of his own fuel or starting his tractor to pull them out.

He loves to tell jokes and have a good time. He's a man who loves life and immerses himself in it. Not wanting to miss a minute of it, he lives each day as fully as he can. He lives hard and plays hard, but he's also a man with frequent lascivious thoughts, which he often verbalizes, a womanizer, and in the later part of his life, an alcoholic too.

Mom always likes to keep informed about what is going on in the world, who is going to be our new prime minister, and what is happening in the community too. When the evening draws to an end Mom likes to relax with a cup of coffee or tea while reading true life and newsworthy stories from her Reader's Digest. She has a quiet demeanor accented by a non-projecting voice she can't make louder no matter how hard she tries. For the most part though, she is always busy doing, and never has much time for being. A fear of judgment, perhaps also a residue of her childhood experiences has taken up residence in her back pocket, and seems to follow her through life.

Her appearance, how she looks, and what others think of her is as important to her as a Bible to the Pope. Whether she is weeding the garden or bringing supper to the men in the field, she always looks as if she has just walked out of the hairdresser or a fashion magazine. One can pretty much eat off the kitchen floor or use the toaster as a mirror to smooth your hair or apply your make-up. Perhaps it is through such things that she derives a sense of security and control.

When I am old enough to hold my balance, my dad often gets me to stand in the palm of his lowered left hand. He raises his right hand palm side up so I can rest my hand in his for extra balance, then he dances around the room and hums a song that makes me feel like I am the best thing since cream cheese. When I turn into a teenager, Dad turns into a teacher. He teaches me how to shoot muskrats that find their way into our pond, how to drive the car, the truck, and the tractor.

Mom is the one who shows me how to plant a garden, husk corn, shell peas, dig out the potatoes, cut the grass, and keep a house clean. When I am little and she waxes the floors with paste wax, I sit on her mop as she pulls and pushes, and twirls me around until the two of us have polished the floor good enough to see our reflection in it. When I am older, she and I take pleasure in sitting kitty corner from each other at the kitchen table where we engage in some arm wrestling contests. We laugh at how red our faces turn with the exertion of trying to force our opponent's hand down first and declare ourselves the champion for the day.

Mom and Dad often go to what is called "Amateur Nights" or "Soirée d'amateur," where people from surrounding communities gather and share their various talents as well as dance, and have a good time. On one such night, about midway through the performances there is a square dance for which my dad gets up, makes his way to the stage, and calls the moves. I stand at the end of the row where I'd been sitting with my mom and watch. I am mesmerized by the rhythm and clap my hands to the beat. I am three years old.

The next performance is someone playing a lively toe-tapping piece on a violin. My dad has shown me how to jig at home, and all that lively music and everyone tapping their feet and clapping their hands gets the best of me. I bolt. I run down the aisle and up the steps to the stage where I join the violin player. The music coming from the violin and the rhythm of the people clapping and tapping their feet to the beat becomes part of my soul. I am completely oblivious to the live audience; I become one with the moment and my feet break into a jig.

The story, as my dad tells it, is that everyone in the audience laughs and claps and are moved by the spontaneity and free spirit of a child to grasp the moment and make it her own. My dad has a smile a mile wide. My mom is embarrassed and horrified. It puts her in the spotlight where she doesn't want to be. People will be talking. What will they say, what will they think and how will this reflect on her? She urges my dad to go get me and bring me back to my seat. When I get there, I don't know what I've done wrong, but I know she isn't very happy, and I get the feeling that it's not okay to lose myself in the moment and listen to the rhythm of my soul.

As a young child, when Dad drinks, I live in terror. I fear the unknown, fear someone getting hurt, and I fear what will happen between Mom and him. I cringe if he makes fun of her or puts her down and makes her feel less than, I fear how he will react when she tries to tell him to stop doing something, or that he's had enough to drink. I have to keep Mom safe, stay with her, and protect her. My job is to change the subject or quickly make the situation lighter somehow.

I remember one time when we're at the beach, Dad gets drunk and falls asleep on top of the picnic table, and the next morning, clad only in his shorts, he runs barefoot through the bushes chasing a bear away from camp. There are other times when Dad can barely walk, and I try to talk him out of getting behind the wheel and taking off to who knows where. Sometimes it works, and sometimes it doesn't.

When he stays home and it is time for me to go to bed, I crawl under the blankets, hold the pillow over my head and stick my fingers in my ears so I won't hear what is happening downstairs.

If I hear him stumble and fall, my imagination takes off on me like a race car. It spins with all kinds of thoughts that maybe he has hurt himself or that, God forbid, he could even be dead. I huddle under the blankets, and talk to myself or make humming noises to drown out the noise from downstairs, and pray that sleep will come, but it doesn't. It never does.

The next day it is business as usual. No one talks about anything that has happened the night before. Sometimes I question if I have imagined it, or if it was all a bad dream since life for Mom and Dad seems to pick up and go on as if nothing ever was.

I am a little more disconnected, a little more distant, a little more lost. I know it doesn't have to be this way, and the craving to live the connections I envisioned at my window embeds a notch deeper in my soul.

Dear One:

What happens to people when they drink?
Who they were disappears and goes away.
Where do they go?
I know I don't imagine what happens.
I also know that's not the way it's supposed to be. There's another way.
I just know it and I need to find it.
No matter what, I'm not going to give up!
I love Mom and Dad and I know they love me but....something is missing.
I'm going to find what's missing. I need to find it for me.
Lou

Chapter 6

The Body Speaks Up

Truth is addictive. Once we taste truth, we hunger to bring more of it into our life.

I'm not sure how it started but I know how it ended—in a silence that spoke louder than words. Like most things that have to do with my body, it is another notch carved into the totem pole of secrecy—a totem that is now towering above me and dares me to break the silence and speak my words. But the only words I hear are the same ones that keep playing in my head from what seems like the very beginning of time, *"Hush little baby, don't say a word...."*

Cindy and I have known each other since we were six years old. We are only a few months apart in age, go to different schools and are opposites in many ways. Cindy is a town girl, squirmy about bugs and mosquito bites, delicate, and on the graceful side. I am the rugged farm girl, a little pipsqueak in ponytails and blue jeans. I love to be outside, snuggle with animals, and climb trees.

We like each other, Cindy and I. We often play pretend games. One day we are acrobats in a circus and the next day or the same afternoon, we are acting out the characters from the Saturday matinee.

As we get older and a little more creative, we make up our own pretend games, and we often play in the loft of the old barn where Dad stores the straw bales for our cows. We climb the wooden ladder into the loft where no one can see us.

I sit and lean against the wall of the barn, close to the open doorway where it is easy to spot someone coming. Cindy scoots up inside the open "V" of my legs, leans against my chest, and snuggles into me, and we play what we call our grown up games.

Maybe it starts because Cindy and I watch a movie with provocative romantic scenes. Maybe it is something we hear or read. Maybe it is who I am. Maybe it is all of that, or maybe it is none of that, but it's somewhere around the age of ten or eleven that my body catches me by complete surprise and responds to the moment as if it has a mind of its own. It's as if it is swept by a tidal wave then continues to experience residual tremors and aftershocks. I am taken aback, bewildered, and filled with a strange combination of guilt and a yearning for more. I feel like I've stolen something I'm not supposed to have. Like when I sneak one of Mom's fresh out of the oven cinnamon buns just as I'm walking out the door.

From there, memories play hopscotch in my mind. There are memories where I wrap my arms around her, hold her close, feel the warmth of her body against mine. Memories of how my hands travel under her shirt, and touch and fondle her breasts while I kiss the back of her neck, and whisper sweet seductive words in her ears. Soon, we move against each other, pressing into one another, both of us moaning as the fire of passion grows within us. For me, those are moments when I abandon everything and embrace everything. A duality of do's and don'ts. A place where I feel connection, love, and need, and I never want it to stop.

One day in my parents' camper we pretend we are a couple. We snuggle together on the seats by the kitchen table. I hold Cindy close and get totally lost in the moment of loving and touching someone. I slowly shift my position so I can be on top of her, and I kiss her, gently at first and then more and more passionately. The next thing I know, my body picks up momentum back and forth, back and forth rubbing against hers, hers rubbing against mine, me travelling to what feels like another dimension, my body possessed by some kind of outside force.

My mind fades in and out of memory, making it difficult for me to realize what belongs on the side of fantasy, and what is a solid imprint born out of true experience. I remember how I get lost in the movement, the softness of her body beneath me, the touch of her lips on mine, the tension that builds inside me as dangerous as dynamite and as delicious as cotton candy.

I remember the surprise I feel when my body goes into some kind of spastic attack as if it is possessed by a force over which I have no control. I remember the waves of tingling sensations travelling between my legs and to every square inch of my anatomy.

I remember how I don't want any of it to end. I remember the electrifying current that runs through me, possesses me, takes over my body and brings me to a height of pleasure I have never experienced or imagined before.

I fear it. I question it. I love it. It carries me away before I can utter so much as a whimper of protest, and I have no choice but to give myself to it. I can't deny its existence, can't stop it from happening, nor do I want to.

I hear a faint voice from somewhere in the distance that asks me to stop, but the current running through me is much stronger than the voice. Like the rollercoaster that reaches the top and starts its descent, there is no way to stop.

That is the last time Cindy and I play those games. I don't know if it's she who avoids situations that could lead to what we used to do, or if it's me. All I know is that it is never mentioned, and we never do it again.

There is a tug-of-war inside me. There's a need to embrace and express, to talk about 'what is', but 'what is' gets hushed or denied. The silence devours my words before I can speak them. When something is denied, permission to talk about it is taken away and I start to question my sanity.

If my friend doesn't want to talk about it, does it mean it didn't happen? If I see my dad crawling on the floor and I ask Mom, "Is he drunk?" And the response I get is, "No, no. Everything is fine." Then what I see, and what I think I understand is different than what I hear you say, or not say, so, again the questions come. Questions like, did I really see that, think that, feel that? Am I imagining things? Am I going crazy?

Denial is insidious. Like cancer cells it eats at my insides. How can I discuss what is denied? The door is closed, slammed shut in my face. I am forced to swallow my words and push them underground.

Denial. Fear. Truth. Reality. Confusion. Questioning. It all sits within me like the sand shifting at the bottom of the sea.

I question. What was the connection, the moment of truth, the melding of one into another that I experienced, and that the vision, in different ways, keeps showing me? How is it connected, or is it? What does it mean? How do I bring it into my life and where will it take me?

Dear One:

Uh... I'm not sure how to say or ask this.

I'm not even sure what I want to say or ask but I know you're the only one I can talk to.

Things happened that felt good in my body, but I don't know if it's a good thing.

I'm confused.

I'm not supposed to feel good in my body, am I? My body is supposed to be separate from the real me, isn't it?

But what I felt did feel good, and it felt very real and very important to me, but I can't talk about it—except maybe here in these letters to you. Is that okay? Can I talk to you?

Lou

Chapter 7

On the Edge

We don't trust the "voice" of truth as our deepest truest friend—we always question it. Yet when we listen and trust, there is no suffering; it's easy—only ego says it's hard.

She is 5'3. I am a whole head short of that. She is free with her words. I hold my tongue. She is a daredevil reaching for forbidden fruit. I am the cautious one with an eye cocked towards safety. She exudes and embraces womanhood. I hide any aspect of femininity.

Heather is two years older than I am, but we are in junior high together at South Wood School. We start hanging out together and before we even get used to where our locker is, we're already exchanging favorite books, study notes and phone numbers. People stop and ask us what's so funny or what we're always laughing about so we tell them. "Hey, did you know that as long as there are tests, there will be prayer in schools?" Then all of us are standing in a circle laughing and sharing jokes. When we're not laughing we're knee deep in innocent everyday conversations about how long to boil an egg to more intimate discussions about the new teacher, how cute he is and what's happening in our awakening bodies. I like her a lot. She is as fresh and as real as the breathe going in and out of me. Before Heather, days without sunshine made me want to stay in bed but now every day is full and bright no matter what is going on outside and I feel like a kid at a magic show.

Shortly after we start grade nine, the magic spell is threatened. Heather's family decides to move to Edmonton, which is a five or six-hour drive from where we live now. Devastated, we concoct a plan.

We plead our case to both sets of parents. My siblings have left home and there is an extra room upstairs. She can live at my place and that way she will get to finish her school year here. It will be a lot better for her to move at the end of junior high, and it will give her parents time to settle into their new home and look for a school for her to attend next year. She will be company for me while my parents go to Kelowna. We can look after the place together. We can help each other out with our homework. Everyone will be happier and it will be a win-win situation for everyone. We rest our case.

To our surprise, it works. Our parents agree to let her come and live at my house until the end of the school year in late June.

Had they given us front row tickets to a live Beatles or Elvis performance, we couldn't be happier. We are thrilled beyond words. I will no longer be alone all the time. I will have someone to connect with and someone to do things with. Although I enjoy being alone, I am starting to realize just how important having someone to share with is meaningful to me.

Heather is a kind, generous, warm-hearted, down-to-earth person who lives life immersed in the moment. Every day starts and ends with a laugh. She teaches me about being present in each moment, about spontaneity, and the sometimes fearful and sometimes rewarding result of stepping out of a person's comfort zone. Through her, I learn how important it is for me to listen to my heart but most important, I learn how a deep connection to another is rewarding and essential to my being.

On the whole, we are good kids. We are responsible and we don't do anything extremely wrong, but when my parents are gone to Kelowna for an extended period of time we take risks that can go sideways.

One day we decide to go into Inspector Clouseau mode and tiptoe around the house sniffing out every nook and cranny determined to find my dad's stash of moonshine. Another time, we decide to walk to the theater ten miles away and chance finding a ride back home when the movie lets out.

The most risky situation however is Heather's innocent flirtatious behavior with two married men. One of the guys is a rancher/cowboy. I go to his place to ride his horses. The other guy is a junior high teacher who is fairly new at our school. For Heather, it starts out as an innocent fun thing but before we know it, the teacher is buying her gifts and showing up at our house when my parents are gone.

He is obsessed with her voluptuous body and trying to see how far he can take things with her. The pressure and the danger mounts. We put our heads together to come up with a way to end this horror before the pot boils over and we get scalded. The next day, both Heather and I seek him out at school. Heather speaks first. "The neighbor," she says, "has spotted your car driving into our place and has asked us why you were there. We had to smooth things out with a story of having borrowed some of your notes to study with and said that you had dropped by to pick them up since you were on your way to Peace River."

I add to what Heather has already said. "Our response seems to have satisfied our neighbor and put an end to her questions, but we can't risk you coming to our place and someone seeing you again."

He agrees. He knows it's a huge risk and he has way too much at stake to push this any further. However, it's not the end for me.

The truth is they are not the only ones obsessed with Heather. I am too. I sit on the edge of her bed and ask her a million questions about everything and anything. I try to innocently prolong my time with her until she undresses and I can admire her drop-dead goddess-like body. I want to reach out and feel her smooth, velvety skin next to mine.

When I am fortunate enough to catch a glimpse of her nakedness, my insides turn to mush. Little explosions start in my chest area and travel all the way down to my groin. Those are times when I swallow hard, talk faster, and desperately try to calm myself down so she won't be aware of what I live inside.

I don't want her to know what is going on for me and have it get in the way of our friendship. I can't let anything jeopardize or sever the deep connection I feel with her, and that she seems to share with me. This connection is much more important than any desires my body has or feels.

When grade nine ends, Heather joins her family in Edmonton, and for a while, life seems pointless, dry, and as bleak and desolate as the prairie land after six or seven months of a cold hard winter.

When September rolls around, instead of going back to the same school, I make the decision to go to Fairview College, a couple hours away from home, to begin my high school studies.

While there, I feel lost, separate, and alone, but I tell no one. After completing one year in the residential program at college, I know this isn't right for me and I choose to go back to my local school to complete my grade eleven and twelve. The school no longer feels the same.

I still see her image everywhere, and every time I walk down the hallway or go to class, my heart hurts for what I once shared with her. I long to have a close, fun, deep, meaningful, and open relationship like I had with Heather, but I can't find that kind of connection with anyone else. All the girls are interested in relationships with guys. This, I am being told in so many different ways is the way it "should be."

Needing to feel connected to others and to have deep meaningful relationships, I try to shift my attention and focus on what "should be."

Dear One:

I don't understand.

I feel things in my gut, and when I feel things in my gut, I know they are real. I know they are true. Yet, what I feel on the inside doesn't always show up on the outside.

Again, that confuses me.

I don't like the feeling of being separate from. I don't like the feeling of not being whole.

If something can feel so right, so real, so genuine with certain things, people and situations, then why can't it exist anytime, anywhere with everyone and everything?

Someone told me that breathing out, and breathing in are two separate things, but that one can't exist without the other. I want to feel connected that way. I want to feel like I am part of a whole. I felt that with Heather. I felt her and I were part of the whole.

Lou

Chapter 8

Wet Girl Promises

When we listen carefully, we can hear the whispers of our soul.

The first time I meet Brad is at the end of our grade-nine school year. Heather and I are attending the annual harvest celebration. Organizers of the event have brought in entertainment suitable for young and old. This time, there is something we have never seen before. A dunk tank is set up as a fundraiser for one of the community resources.

My friend and I watch as fully clothed daring individuals take turns to sit on a little platform suspended over the pool. Once they are perched high above the water, people purchase baseballs to throw at the target. If they hit the target, it releases the bar holding the platform, and down goes the person into the water below.

Both of us watch and laugh at the surprised look on people's faces as they hit the water. Even if they know it is going to happen, nobody seems to quite expect it when it does. It doesn't take long for people in the crowd to be pulled into the fun of it and start making bets on how many balls it will take before the person goes down. That's about the time my friend turns to me and says, "I dare you."

"Dare me to what?" I ask.

"I dare you to go up there," she says.

Never one to let a good dare go by, I promptly empty my pockets and up the ladder I go. A couple of people come by and try, but lucky for me, miss the target. I have a good view from my perch and a smug look on my face as I smile at the people below. Then it is his turn.

A tall redhead with a leather jacket purchases three balls, steps up to the mark in front of the target takes his jacket off, and sets it on the ground beside him.

"Hmmm… mean business do you?" I ask.

"Sure do," he responds. "You ready?"

And with those words his right foot and right arm swing back, then he lunges forward and releases the ball dead on target, and down I go.

A little cheezed off at getting dunked by his first throw, I shake the water from my hair and haul myself right back up the ladder once more. With a smile on his face as wide as a rainbow, the tall redhead picks up another ball, yells, "Ready?" and takes another swing at the target. Before I can even get any words out of my mouth, down I go again. This time I stand up even quicker, wipe the water from my eyes, and determined to see him miss, stamp back up the ladder. I am still getting myself into a sitting position when he throws his last ball and hits dead on target for the third time in a row.

Enough already! I pull myself out of the water and my friend comes to join me. We start to walk away, both of us laughing and joking about what just happened and at the squishy sucking sounds, my feet are making in my shoes as we make our way down the sidewalk. Then we hear;

"Hey there, wet girl!"

I turn to see who has spoken, and there he is on his motorbike, hugging the edge of the sidewalk, following us around and trying to get me to pay attention to him.

I look straight ahead and ignore him. I pretend he isn't there. He persists. He keeps following. "Hey, wet girl, what's your name? Can I give you a ride on my bike to wherever you're going? Can I get you a towel?" I keep walking. He keeps following.

In a weird sort of way, with Heather foremost on my mind, I suppose I could say, I have my first date with Brad, on a sunny afternoon in the midst of a community celebration—and that's how it all starts in a fun kind of way, but not at all how it ends.

Brad and I start seeing more of each other. I am fourteen years old. He is sixteen. We are two teenagers who fall in love, perhaps not so much with each other as with the magic of the moment and what "should" be.

Two years later, my finger is adorned with an engagement ring. The following year, when I am seventeen and Brad is nineteen, we get married at our local church surrounded by sixty family members and friends who come to witness our wedding vows. We are young and in love, or so we think, but we have no idea what love really is.

I am excited for this special day, but I don't give much thought to the seriousness of what I am getting into. I am like a puppet on a string going along with the motions of what comes next. It's like how after you eat dinner, you wash the dirty dishes, and after you wash the dirty dishes, you rinse the soap off of them, and after you rinse the soap off of them, you wipe them dry. One step leads to the next step, because that's what you're supposed to do. I follow the steps all the way to the end.

And so it is that the first time I have sex with a man is the day I walk out of church with a piece of paper that confirms I am now officially married. Then, just like that, what before marriage was a wrongdoing, suddenly becomes not only permissible but also expected. According to parents, society, and church rules and regulations, I am now licensed to go all the way.

Here I am, a ninety-five pound seventeen year-old, mature enough for my age, but still unsure of who I am, and barely old enough to stand on the threshold of adulthood. I anticipate this act of consummation to be a life altering experience from which I will never want to return. It isn't.

Perhaps it's the experimenting in parked cars that has created a greater expectation in my mind. Perhaps it's the signed piece of paper giving the green light that leads to much shorter foreplay than I am used to. Or perhaps, it is my expectation of capturing the same feeling I experience in the vision of the five-year-old. The feeling of deep connection and of being 'One' with the other that I am looking for, but I am left feeling like when I go to the store and I'm not sure what I want, or I forgot what I came for, and I wander around the aisles looking and feeling at a loss for something without being able to name what it is.

When Brad and I get back from our week-long honeymoon, we move into an 8 x 10 holiday trailer, and within a month, I discover I am pregnant. There is no room for a baby in our tiny space so we decide to build an 8 x 10 addition to our existing mobile. At the time of this pregnancy, Brad is working as a produce manager at the local IGA, and I am working in the administration office at the hospital in a neighboring town. I work until I am close to the end of my pregnancy, then I quit my job. At eighteen, I give birth to our son, Kevin.

Our marriage is an unsettled one from the beginning and I try to figure out why. Maybe an immediate pregnancy doesn't give us time to adjust to each other and changes things for us in ways that proves to be detrimental to our relationship. Maybe it is more than we are ready for. Maybe sexual, emotional, and physical needs are all messed up like a tangled ball of yarn. Maybe we are too young and immature, too blind, insecure, and ill equipped to know how to make an intimate relationship work, much less what it means to have the added responsibility of raising a child. I hate to admit it to myself, but my doubts about us grow and it doesn't take long before I've got more questions dancing around in my head than I know what to do with.

What we know about matters of the heart, about two people sharing their lives together or raising children is about as much as a city raised kid knows about driving a combine at harvest time. We haven't learned how to reach down to where the real stuff is and grab the words that are needing to be said. We float around on the surface and stick to saying safe familiar words like "I love you," without paying attention to the despondent look on our face or how our body slumps forward or pulls away. Then, instead of picking up a needle and thread we let things slip by hoping they will somehow magically disappear. They don't.

In the first year of our marriage, Brad continues his role as president of a local youth center. I attend a few of the sponsored dances with him, but I am pregnant and feel awkward and out of place at functions with teens who live a different life than we do. Brad loves what he does and sees no reason to put an end to it.

I feel lonely and confused. I have no idea about hormone changes that occur as a result of pregnancy, or what to expect when giving birth, except for the little bit I read in books. I know I'm more sensitive and emotional than before, but whether it is a result of being pregnant, or a result of the way our relationship is, or a combination of both, I'm not sure. What I do know is that the house, as small and as crowded as it is, feels big and empty. I look out the window and see two teenagers holding hands and another couple who are biking down the street talking and smiling at each other. I see what I am estranged from and for the moment, feels out of my reach.

Brad and I hardly see each other, and when we do, it's not good. After our day's work during the week as well as weekends, Brad makes his way to the youth center. I go for walks and sometimes, even though I feel uncomfortable with my big belly, pop into the youth center. When I do, I often find him on the dance floor dancing with a girl, both of them hanging on to each other like there was a piece of Velcro between them. He comes home in the early morning hours claiming he has to stay until the end so he can lock up after everyone else has gone home.

There is no one I feel I can talk to about my doubts and fears about my relationship, or the anticipation of becoming a mom and the ups and downs of my pregnancy. I can see our marriage disintegrating before my eyes, and I have no idea what to do about it, or how to make it better.

One night, when I am around five months pregnant and my husband is again at the youth center, the loneliness gets so bad it feels like the world is caving in. I am suffocating. I grab the keys; squeeze my belly behind the wheel of the car.

I drive down some country roads with no idea where I am going. I drive slowly at first. My knuckles are turning white from my grip on the steering wheel. My elbows are locked in place and the muscles in my shoulders are taut with fear as I ram my foot down on the accelerator. The car spins and swerves to the left then to the right and back again. Gravel spits out from beneath the tires like little hand grenades and I am swallowed by a cloud of dust. I get a flash image of the car hitting the ditch at this speed or going over an embankment and smashing into a million pieces. A thought zips across my mind. This will be the end of it, and everyone will think it was an accident. No one will know any different. Just like that, in one split second, all the pain will go away.

The steering wheel spins this way and that way and the car starts tilting to one side. I brace myself. Then, boom! I get kicked in the ribs. I lift my foot off the accelerator and slam my foot down on the brake, spin in the opposite direction and come to a dead stop. Oh my God, the baby!

I make a promise to both of us.

Dear One:

Last night I went to sleep with my fingers intertwined and my hands cradling the underside of my protruding belly.

I felt the little movements inside me. The life that perhaps saved mine and reminded me of the vision of connection and love I saw as a child.

I want to live that. I don't know how.

Lou

Chapter 9

A New Life

To get to truth we have to be able to dismantle the false beliefs of the ego.

When I go into labor in the early morning hours of August 25th, Brad takes me to the hospital and stays with me until I am wheeled into the delivery room around one in the afternoon. Then like other expectant fathers, he paces the hallways and waits to hear the results.

I am eighteen years old and about as green about childbirth as a new sapling poking through the forest floor. The delivery room looks like an alien spacecraft with all its bright lights, flashing monitors, oxygen tanks, various coiled tubes and pipes. Two nurses with masks that cover most of their faces stand on either side of me.

I feel panicky like a rabbit caught in the headlights not knowing where to run. My body shakes as if suffering from hypothermia. I dig my fingers into the arm of the young Filipino nurse to my right and plead with her, "Don't leave me, okay?"

"Don't worry. I'm not going anywhere," she reassures me. A couple of minutes later the door to the delivery room opens followed by the familiar sound of feet shuffling on the floor. Doc Fiske, the same doctor who brought me into the world some eighteen years earlier has arrived. This reassures me and helps me calm down.

"Well, young lady," he says, as he peers over his half glasses. "Apparently you're in a hurry to bring this child into the world. I didn't even have time to grab dessert."

"Let me make it my treat when we're done here," I respond.

"You're on," he says as he proceeds to give the nurses instructions.

I glance at the huge black and white clock on the wall to my left. It is 1:45 pm. Fifteen minutes later, after six hours of intense back labor, I hear Doc Fiske say, as enthusiastically as if it was his own child he helped bring into the world, "It's a boy!"

His words are like music to my ears. The miracle of a new life entering the world has just taken place and I am part of that miraculous process. I am a mom!

"Is he all right?" I ask.

In answer to my question, and even before he cuts the cord, Doc Fiske reaches over, lays the baby on my stomach, and says, "Here you go. Meet your son, and yes, he's just fine."

I can't believe my eyes. There he is, a beautiful, healthy baby boy who is as blond as blond can be! Nothing can compare with the love and connection I feel in this moment and have never felt before. Tears of joy run down my face, as I kiss and cuddle my son lying across my breast, our hearts beating as *One*.

When they wheel me out of the delivery room, Brad comes to meet me and takes my hand in his. "We have a son," I tell him. "We have a son." Brad comes with me to my room, the nurses bring the baby, and he holds him for the first time. The smile on his face makes me cry. There is no doubt about it. He is proud to be a dad. I lay back down to rest. I am exhausted.

After about an hour or so, Brad leaves the hospital to go tell everyone the good news, and comes back around five that evening to spend some time with the baby and me, and then leaves again by seven. There is a function at the youth center. I open my mouth to say something. I turn towards the window and a tear rolls across the bridge of my nose onto the pillow. I watch the day slip into the night.

In the first year of our marriage, things unfold in such a way that in the evenings and on weekends Brad continues to "manage" the youth club. I stay home and "manage" cleaning, laundry, cooking, and a colicky baby. For the first few months of his life, Kevin wails and cries, and I rock him back and forth and pace the floor with him. For every ounce of breast milk that goes into him, I swear two ounces come back out. On nights when nothing works to calm him down, I bundle him up and take him for a car ride hoping the movement will help him to quiet down and fall asleep.

On such a night, I find myself in a neighboring town circling a friend's house where many of my old school buddies I've known since grade school have gathered. I envy them and I feel a desperate need to connect with them. I know that Jacques, my childhood sweetheart is going to be there, and even though I know I probably shouldn't, something within me needs to connect with all my friends and with Jacques's kind, beautiful, soft-spoken soul.

My thoughts flip back to how he's the first person I saw when I walked into church the day I married Brad. Jacques and Marcel sat in the back pew waiting for me to arrive. When I walked in wearing my long white wedding gown, tears filled Jacques's eyes, and it felt as if he was pleading with me, "Please, don't do this."

In that instant, time stood still. I looked at the tears in Jacques's eyes then looked at Brad who was standing at the front of the church waiting for me to walk down the aisle. I was afraid I was making a huge mistake, but it was too late to do anything about it. My knees started to buckle beneath me and my heart pounded against my chest, echoing in my ears. From somewhere deep inside me, I heard a voice saying, "What are you doing?"

I froze. I was unable to move. I wanted to go backwards in time, but I felt a tug on my arm urging me forward. My dad was giving me the signal. People were waiting. It was time to walk down the aisle. I took a deep breath and inched forward. My feet were weighed down, my steps mechanical. I passed Jacques and looked ahead at Brad who stood at the end of the aisle waiting for me. I chased away the thoughts that raced through my mind, cleared my head, and focused on the present moment, and what I was here to do.

I didn't have the guts to walk out. I didn't have a choice. I had to do the "right" thing, and "not" bring shame. I swallowed hard and hung on to my dad's arm. When I walked out of church on Brad's arm, Jacques had disappeared.

I give my head a shake to bring myself back to the present moment and find I am parked. Kevin is asleep. I can see my friends through the living room window. I pick up my son and make my way to the front door. One of my friends comes to greet me. When she sees that Kevin is asleep, she leads me to the bedroom where I can put Kevin down so he won't be disturbed.

It is great to see everyone. Things are different now and as much as I want to be there, I know I shouldn't be.

When I go into the bedroom to get my son, Jacques follows me. "How is your baby doing? Can I see him?"

I pull the blankets away from Kevin's face. "He looks like a little angel sleeping so peacefully," he says. Then he turns to me and asks, "And how are you doing? Are you okay?"

I start to cry. He reaches out for me, holds me in his arms, wipes my tears, and whispers in my ear, "Shhh, shhh… everything will be alright." Then he kisses me and I let him.

At some point, from somewhere deep inside, we find the strength to pull away from each other. I pick up my son, walk out, and make my way to my car. That is the last time I see Jacques until both of us are in our late thirties.

By the time Kevin is six months old, the colic has tamed down, and I go back to work in order to supplement our income. I apply for whatever part-time jobs become available. One of the jobs I get is working in the concession at the movie theater, which is owned by friends of my parents. A few months after I start working for them, they approach Brad and me with a proposition. They are looking for a way to retire, and they want to offer us the opportunity to buy the two hundred and fifty seat theater. They offer us a rental purchase agreement, payable over a five-year period. We are thrilled to be given this opportunity, and jump in.

In the beginning, Brad continues to work his day job, and in the evening, he is being trained to operate the projectors. We sell our humble little home and move into what seems like a huge two-bedroom apartment situated on the top floor of the theater. Next to our apartment is a connecting door to the projection room. On the ground floor, next to the theater entrance, there is another huge room that is already rented out for use as a barbershop. We can barely believe our luck. This is the perfect opportunity for us to get on our feet financially and earn a living while working towards owning our own business. This, I think, will change our lives forever. It does, but not at all the way I think it will.

What follows are a couple of years filled with adjustments, of dreams being built, dreams shattering, and dreams evaporating like dew in the morning sun. Brad works upstairs operating the projectors. I work downstairs selling admission tickets and overseeing the employees in the concession area. We are busy and completely immersed in finding ways to make our new business successful.

A few months into the operation of our business, the barber who is renting downstairs decides to close shop and move out. That's when Brad decides to quit his day job as a produce manager and venture into yet another business. With his continued interest in motorbikes, he decides to use the barbershop space as a storefront to sell motorbikes as well as motorized all-terrain vehicles, better known as quads, to hunters and sports enthusiasts. With this new project, his involvement with the youth club starts to diminish, and although things are far from perfect, I feel things are going better for us. I choose to concentrate on the positive moments and how we are moving forward in building a life for ourselves. I fail to see, or maybe refuse to see, what is happening right under my nose.

Dear One:

I am grateful for the opportunity to build a life for ourselves. It has given Brad and me more time together. In some ways, we are more connected—well, when it comes to our business and how to run it that is. I feel like I am a part of and belong more since we are both part of this together. I'm not so sure it's made any difference on how open, kind and loving we are to each other like nothing else was more important in the world.

Sometimes I wonder if maybe I'm living in a dream world and there's no such thing as communication beyond words. I want a connection that is a felt experience more so than one that is spoken or demonstrated. Is there such a thing?

Yet, even as I ask, I know. I know there is. I've seen it. I've felt it. I swear I'll find it. I have to.

Lou

Chapter 10

Arriving and Leaving

In the face of truth, the question, "Is this right?" becomes obsolete.
I just know.

We never made a conscious decision to have our first child, but when our business starts doing well and things look good for us financially, we discuss having a second child.

Maybe, we think another baby will smooth out the rough edges. Maybe we hope another child will somehow magically make things better. Maybe it is just me fooling myself. In any case, not long after our discussion, I am pregnant with our second child.

Life settles into a fairly normal way of life. Both the theater and bike shop business are doing well, and so, I think, are we. But while the child inside me grows, other things are picking up momentum and growing too.

No matter how I try to hang on to the dream, it soon becomes obvious that I am trying to hang on to a marriage that is disintegrating and crumbling around me like a house built on sand.

"Is there something you'd like to talk about? Something you're not telling me that I should know maybe?"

Brad turns towards the TV to turn the volume up a notch and stares into the screen. "Why do you always think there is something to talk about. I swear you imagine things."

I start to think I am an overreacting, jealous, young wife, but little by little, I feel the tugging of an undertow taking me further and further away from shore. Brad's involvement with the youth center has greatly diminished, but I still feel an underlying uneasiness that I can only describe as a steady mist permeating my otherwise sunny days.

Over the next few months, the mist thickens, the undertow gets stronger, and I feel more and more unsettled about our relationship. The air between us is tense and my stomach feels like I have constant indigestion. Brad is spending more hours downstairs in his bike shop. He works later into the night, makes more frequent trips to the coffee shop, drops in more often at the youth club, and visits the farm where his brother and sister-in-law live more than he's ever done before.

What is going on? Is this normal? Is this what marriage is like? Whom can I ask? Whom can I talk to? The friends I have are involved in our business, or are related in some way, and I don't feel I can confide in them. We have no young couples our age we hang around with, because in the evenings when others go out, we are busy at the theater. It is just Brad and me with no compass to point the way.

In September of 1972, a little over a year after taking over the theater, when I am twenty years old, our second child comes into the world. Brad calls his sister to come and look after Kevin while he takes me to the Peace River hospital, which is an hour away. He stays with me until I go through admissions and I am brought to my room, then he goes back home to look after his motorbike business and prepare for the evening movie. Later that evening, I call to let him know we have a beautiful healthy daughter and we are both doing fine. The next day he comes to the hospital to meet Karen.

A few days later, I am given the okay to go home,. Brad won't come because there's no one to look after the bike shop or theater. Calling my sisters isn't an option either as one of them lives in BC and the other one in Quebec. I call my brother Richard's house knowing my sister-in-law will come for me.

Things seem to go well when I get back home, or maybe it's because I am busier than usual and have less time to notice the undertow. My days are full with the care of our daughter and our two year-old son, looking after the household, doing the bookwork for the theater business, ordering films, confectionary supplies, tickets and whatever general upkeep and cleaning of the building Brad doesn't have time to do.

By the spring of 1973, when Karen is about six months old, things puzzle me, and I start to question. I notice changes in Brad's attitude. He starts closing his bike shop more often to go service bikes. At about the same time as this is happening, I start to receive phone calls at home. If I answer, the line goes dead. When Brad answers, there is a brief conversation, or he takes the phone to another room. Then in the evening, after the theater closes and I see him reach for his jacket, I ask, "Where are you going now?"

"I need a break. Geez! I'm just going out for coffee with friends."

The uneasiness in the pit of my stomach grows. Am I imagining things? Every day I try to convince myself I am reading too much into things, but the doubts and fears I have experienced in the first year of our marriage resurface, and play havoc with my mind.

Then one night, about half way through the movie, and at about the time when I usually tell the person working in concession she can leave for the evening, I decide to ask her if she can stay a little bit longer so I can go upstairs to do a few things. I don't know what tells me I need to go upstairs, but I let my intuition guide me.

I start up the staircase. Each step I take feels heavy like cresting the top of a mountain where there's barely any oxygen. I creep up the steps quietly but purposefully. Something tells me to move forward in order to find truth. I reach the top stairs and step onto the landing by the projection room door. I hold my breath, listen and hear voices on the other side. At first, I think it is voices from the movie but then I recognize my husband's voice and shortly after, I hear a female voice too. I freeze like a mannequin in a department store window. My legs feel weak and my insides turn to mush. In that instant, the lies I have told myself are exposed.

After what feels like an eternity, but likely only seconds, I raise my hand to gently push the projection door open. It doesn't move. The door is locked. If I have one smidgen of hope left that my suspicions will be proven wrong, in that brief moment, all of it disappears along with any traces of dreams yet to come.

I take a deep breath and with bile in my throat, I hear some resemblance of my voice ask to be let in. There are audible gasps and a sense of panic coming from the other side and Brad's voice comes back to mock me. "I'm busy," he says.

"I'm sure you are," I respond. "Either I make a scene for the whole theater and three blocks around to hear me, or you open the door now."

The lock turns. I push the door open and peer into the dim lit room and there is my husband standing next to a fourteen-year-old girl. Both appear to be in complete disarray. I stand there for a few moments and stare at their images which dance and flicker in the dim light of the projectors. The movie reels turn and the life on the screen roar on while my own life disintegrates in front of my eyes.

I stare at them for a moment. Tears roll down my face as I turn and silently make my way back down the stairs. I go to the bathroom, wash my face in cold water and walk back to the concession booth to tell my employee she is free to go home now. She leaves. I look at the clock. It is 9:15 pm; the movie is finishing at 10 pm. I have another forty-five minutes to wait. Wait for what? To face Brad again? For my marriage to end? For someone to come and tell me I am dreaming and life will go on?

After everyone files out of the theater and I finish what I have to do, I go look for Brad and realize he has already left. Our Chevy truck is gone. I stay up and wait for his return. In the middle of the night, as I sit on the couch with my baby snuggled in my arms sucking at my breast, I stare at the stars out the living room window. I think of myself as the five-year-old looking out my bedroom window, being immersed in a vision of deep connection and *Oneness*, and it feels so far away and distant.

I watch the clock as every minute ticks by and the minutes turn into an hour, then another and another. I pace the floor trying to figure out where to go with all this. Then suddenly it comes to me. I know exactly what I have to do.

Through all the confusion and turmoil one thing becomes absolutely clear. I have to leave. There is no way I can do this anymore. I cannot, will not, spend even one more night like this. Images come to my mind of my mom sick with worry about where my dad is or what he is up to when he fails to come home at night, and I know with certainty that I cannot, and will not, do that. I will not go through nights of wondering where my husband is. Wondering if he is injured in an accident or spending the evening wrapped in someone else's arms while I sit at home and hold down the fort, take care of the kids, bite my nails, and burn holes in my stomach with worry and grief.

I look at the clock again. It is 5:30 am. I tiptoe into Kevin and Karen's room and pack a bag for each of them, and then go to our bedroom and pack a bag for myself. I jump in the shower and try to wash away the hurt and sadness that has settled into my heart.

I step out of the shower determined to step forward into the future and not look back. I get dressed, go to the desk and open the books to our joint bank account. We have a little over $5,000 in savings. I think about it for a minute. He is gone with the only vehicle we have, a pickup worth about the same amount of money. I take my pen, write myself a check for $5000 and put it in my pocket. I glance at the clock again. It is just after 6.00 am. Close enough. I pick up the phone and call.

A sleepy voice comes on at the other end. "Hello."

"It's Lou," I say. I hear some movement at the other end of the line as my sister-in-law, the one who picked me up from the hospital after Karen was born, sits up in bed.

"Are you okay?" she asks with obvious concern in her voice.

"I'm okay," I respond. "Well, actually I'm not. I'm leaving Brad. The kids and I need a ride. Can you come and pick us up? Can I go to your place for now? I don't know where else to go."

"Oh my goodness! When do you want me to come?" she asks.

"We're ready to go now."

Dear One:

I don't know if anyone out there will understand what I'm doing.

I don't know where I'll find the strength to follow through.

I need to feel like I am One. Not alone and separate from.

Please......stand by me if you can.

Lou

Chapter 11

A Sharp Left Turn

Truth allows us to move forward because all the lies and all the fluff fall away and the path becomes clear.

The following afternoon, my brother Richard has set up his holiday trailer next to their house so I can stay there with the kids until I decide what to do and where to go. When I unpack the kid's bags, I realize I have forgotten some things they need and can't be without, and I will have to make a trip back to my house to pick them up.

I borrow Richard's vehicle and drive to town, but when I get to the house, I am flooded with anxiety at the reality of my situation. What the hell am I doing leaving my home and my life with two kids and no clue where I'm going and what I'm going to do? I make a silent plea. Please God, I ask, please give me the strength to do what I need to do, and to go through with this.

I walk up the steps that lead to our apartment and as I get closer I hear music coming from inside. Brad doesn't listen to music. Someone else is in there, in my bedroom playing my music on my stereo. I feel like someone has thrown a match to my acid filled stomach.

I grab the doorknob and turn. The door is locked. I try to peek through the window on the door, but the semi-transparent curtain I swore I would get rid of and never did, makes it difficult for me to make out the shadows moving around inside. I knock, then I pound with my fist and scream, "Open the damn door." There is no response. Then I realize I still have my key. I pull it out of my pocket and slip it into the lock. It doesn't work. The lock has been changed. I run down the steps and leave.

A few days later, I find an apartment to move into in a neighboring town, and I let Brad know I am coming to the house to get the children's beds and whatever else I need. Brad is there to open the door, and tells me, "Take whatever you want or need." Then he leaves.

I am hurt, disappointed, and downright pissed off, but later, once I've had time to think it through, I realize that Brad is not the bad person in this marriage and neither am I. What I start to see is that both of us were trying to define who we were and we became a couple before we even knew or came to terms with ourselves as individuals.

I am searching for relationships that so far exist only in a vision that lives in the confines of my heart and mind. The only thing I know for sure is that I have to live in truth and in a place of love. How to live that in real life, I am not sure. But what I am pretty sure of is that it isn't supposed to be a battle, or like standing on the precipice of a deep dark hole. I am not willing to be a participant in this cat and mouse game of deception, and I am not willing to be a third wheel within my own marriage.

When I leave, Brad stays with whatever we have invested in the theater business, his motorcycle shop, a way that he can make a living, our vehicle as well as the freedom to see who he wants and do as he pleases.

Life for him continues and maintains some consistency. Life for my children and me however, throws us into a completely different world. Nevertheless, I know I have what is most important, my two children and my sanity. What I don't know is that my life at twenty is about to take a sharp left turn.

Dear One:

It's not the way it was supposed to go. Not in my mind anyway. I know I made some pretty huge decisions rather hastily and I know a lot of people are shaking their heads. To me the future of this marriage was clearly marked, and it's not a road I am willing to travel. I have no idea about the unknown road ahead, but at least it's one I am choosing instead of being forced to live with someone else's choices.

People are willing to tell me now what they saw. Why not before? Was it a fear of hurting me, him, us, or a fear of not being believed?

Are there different pathways to truth? Are there different situations when it's okay to speak truth and situations when it isn't? What can help us figure it out? What's to guide us when it comes to truth—the discovery of it, the sharing of it and the living of it?

I know it can exist. I saw it in my vision. I just need to find it.

Lou

Chapter 12

A Move & A Rude Awakening

Truth can often humble us and bring us to our knees and truth can fill our heart and make us feel like we are standing on top of the world.

The day I am going back to the house to move some stuff out, I decide to ask an old friend from school if he can come with his truck to help me. The next day, Garry helps me move to an apartment in a neighboring town seven miles west of Falher. When we're done, I breathe a huge sigh of relief, thank Garry for coming to my rescue, and invite him to join me for supper. He politely declines saying he has to get back to the farm to look after the cattle, but that he would like to drop by and visit later. I let him know that I would very much like that.

By the time Garry decides to come for that visit, a little over a month later, I have already cleared the place and gone. When I am unable to find work, I apply for temporary help from welfare and discover that if I register under their umbrella, they will not allow me to take on any work in order to supplement the little income they will provide for my family and me. If I get on their system, there is little hope of breaking free from it, and I am not prepared to live without hope of moving forward, of things getting better.

Calls to my sister Lucie, in Quebec, assure me that there is plenty of work there and I won't have trouble finding a job. I see it as my only solution, and the next day I purchase one-way train tickets to Quebec. It's a three day trip, that will take me and my children across Canada to start a new life for ourselves.

Lucie lives in Buckingham, about twenty-five miles from Ottawa. Within a few days, I find an apartment and a job and I get down to the business of earning a living and raising my children. Sheer stubbornness, determination, and hard work get me through the next couple of years. I work for minimum wage of $2.60 an hour, and from that, I have to pay rent, a babysitter, buy groceries, and maintain a little station wagon I purchased with the five thousand dollars I took when I left Brad.

Most meals are some form of mac and cheese with bologna or wieners. When I can work extra hours and earn extra money, I splurge on hamburger with a treat of cookies and lemonade for the kids. Every week, I count my pennies to make sure that when my days off roll around, I will have enough money to put a few dollars of gas in the car so we can go on outings.

In the summer months, I throw a piece of foam that serves as a mattress, blankets, and whatever else we might need in the back of our Nissan station wagon and off we go to camp at a nearby lake. We sleep in the car and cook on the outside fire pit. We play in the water and bask in the sun. We pick rocks. We draw pictures. We watch the moon grow, and count the stars. We go for walks, examine bugs, and pick leaves, and whatever else we can find. We make good use of the limited time we have together. We are poor in material things, but we are rich in experience and love.

During the summer when temperatures soar in the triple digits and the humidity is high, I can wring out my clothes by the time I get home from work at the grocery store. On one of those long, crazy, hot, busy summer days where I have stocked shelves and heaved heavy cases of beer over the counter to a countless stream of customers heading to the lake, I drag myself home, completely exhausted and worn out. All I want to do when I get home is take a cold shower and put my feet up.

I finally make it home and barely have time to turn the doorknob when my babysitter flies out the door to join her friends who are waiting for her in a car across the street. I step over the threshold into the house and it's as if I've entered a war zone. Kevin and Karen are squabbling over toys in a living room that looks like a tornado has whipped through it. The sink is piled high with dirty dishes. The place looks like a pigsty, and the kid's high-pitched screams and squeals make me want to turn around, walk out, and lock the door behind me. I try to talk to them, hug them, hold them close, and calm things down, but nothing I say or do makes any difference. They scream and wail louder and louder. They just won't shut up.

I should know to pull away, to take some deep breaths, to take a walk around the kitchen or the backyard for a couple of minutes so I can cool off, but it's hard for me to even think as I stand there and feel every last ounce of energy drain out of me. I throw my arms up in the air, and the tap opens as my eyes cloud over with tears, and I too start to cry. Kevin screams louder and Karen follows suit. The noise is deafening. It has to stop. I have to make it stop.

I grab Kevin by the shoulders, shake him, and scream at him. "Shut up, shut up! Shut the hell up!" Then, just as quickly as this horror started, it stops. It is as if someone has dropped a mirror in front of me. I catch an image of myself shaking my son and I am mortified. I want to die. I see an out of control mother and an innocent little child sobbing with tears running down his cheeks and fear emanating from his eyes. I am the one who is supposed to protect him. I am the one who is supposed to take care of him. I am the one person he trusts and I am breaking that trust. I am taking that away from him. In that moment, I hate myself and I want to vomit.

I hear a strange noise, like a cat's cry that comes from somewhere deep inside me. I pull Kevin into my arms, squeeze him next to my chest, pass my hand through his blond, curly hair, kiss him repeatedly and tell him. "Oh, my God, Kevin! Oh, my God! I am so sorry. So very sorry. I didn't mean to do that. I didn't mean to hurt you. Mommy loves you so very much. I'm so, so sorry. I will never do that again. I promise. I will never do that again."

I reach for Karen who has gone quiet and pull her into my arms too. The three of us sit on the living room floor, amongst the wooden blocks, books, toy cars, and coloring books, and we rock each other back and forth back and forth until we have calmed down.

That evening, after the children have gone to bed, the shame of what I've done lingers in my soul and I reach for my journal to try and write my way through it.

Dear One:
How did I abandon my truth?
I look at Kevin and Karen and my heart hurts.
What I've done is completely unacceptable and I am so sorry.
This is one thing I swear will never ever happen again. Never!
Of that, I am absolutely sure.
Lou

Chapter 13

Commitments, Conflicts, Connections

Finding freedom takes longer than grabbing a cookie from the cookie jar.

Once I've have been in my Quebec home and my new job for a while, I decide to write to Garry to let him know how much his kindness meant to me when he came to help me move. We begin a friendly two year correspondence that becomes a little more serious with each letter we exchange. That year, on Valentine's Day, I receive a beautiful card from Garry, the first Valentine I've ever received as an adult, and it touches me deeply.

On several occasions, I invite him to come and visit me in Quebec, and although he indicates he would love to, he adds that he is always too busy on the farm, and admits it would mean stepping way out of his comfort zone. No one in his family has ever travelled much or ventured far from home.

Our letters continue and our correspondence becomes more intimate as we get to know each other better. I decide to move back to Alberta.

On January 16, 1975, Garry and I are married in a private ceremony performed by a United Church minister in Peace River, AB. The only people present are two friends who are there to witness our vows. We purchase a mobile home in Falher and in the spring move it to his mom and dad's farm where we live for the next eight years. Those eight years, in many ways, shape our marriage and our lives.

Garry welcomes my children into his life as his own. However, my arrival on the scene, a divorcee with two children, is not what his parents had in mind for their one and only son. The tension between my mother-in-law and me is often palpable even to a stranger and made evident through her harsh words and tone of voice with me, and my own lack of words and voice with her.

Our mobile home is situated across the driveway facing Garry's parents' home. Our homes are so close together that if our curtains are open we can see into each other's house. I am used to complete independence from my parents with only the occasional visit from them once or twice a year. Garry, on the other hand, is used to being involved with his parents daily which to me feels like there are no boundaries.

My mother-in-law and I do share some good moments and kind gestures, like when she offers to babysit or when I offer to pick up something in town or fix something for her. But there are also some extremely difficult times, and I often feel sorry for Garry who is caught in the middle between his mother and me, and a tension that is hard, if not impossible to appease.

While living in my in-law's yard, I question what is the right way to walk across the yard, the right way to look, the right way to say or do something. I am often crushed by things that are insinuated, said, or done, but I cringe at the thought of creating more conflict plus I don't have the backbone or the voice to stand up for myself, but I have an even stronger determination to find a way to do so.

The worst part is the *Jekyll and Hyde* kind of situation where I never know what is coming next. Sometimes it is a day filled with kind gestures, smiles, and positive words and other days nothing I say or do makes any difference or is right in any way, shape or form. I go from a heart filled with hope to frustration, anger, and tears. Over and over again. I try to discuss with Garry the possibility of moving to a place where we can have a place to call our own, but, because of financial reasons, it takes us another seven years to make that move.

Looking back, I can see that Garry and I never had time alone to nurture our life as a couple. We started our relationship with two children, and within a few months, we moved into his parents' yard, so they became part of our lives right away, and a year or so later our daughter Jody came into our lives, and a year and a half after that, our daughter Brenda was born. With our growing family I can see how from my in-laws perspective, it must have sometimes felt like their yard, time and space was being invaded.

By 1982, having fast outgrown our mobile home, and with finances being a bit better, we take the leap, buy a modular home and move to a farm about half a mile away from his parents' place. Moving there feels like a honeymoon for the first little while. Garry, I notice is more relaxed in setting his own schedule for work and I feel I can breathe easier and am no longer always looking over my shoulder.

I am grateful that his parents could help us get on our feet but I am relieved to have our own space—a place where we can do what we want and finally call home. Having our own place creates a positive shift in our relationship. We talk more and spend more time together.

When the children are little they go to daycare, and I work at part-time jobs outside the home and help with farming as much as I can. As the kids get older and are in school, I work full-time jobs and work on the farm. During harvest, I am the one who does the trucking, hauling the grain from the combine to the farmyard and back again. I operate the grain dryer, swath and drive the tractor, make bales or work the land. It is a busy household, two adults, four kids, two dogs, and always one or two cats or more. When the kids get older, there is the added busyness of having to drive them back and forth to various lessons or practices in town. There is band, swimming, baseball, skating practices and competitions, and sleepovers at friends. Days fly by, and at the end of the day I often drop into bed, only to get up and start all over again the next day.

Dear One:

I just wanted to say how grateful I am to be living in our own place. I love to drive into our yard and feel as if I'm coming home.

Every morning when I look out the window or step out the door, I connect with the nature that surrounds me.

I watch the sunrise wink at me through the trees. Later as the evening comes to a close, I watch it make its descent as it creates a spectacular sunset over the prairie wheat field. I marvel at the open spaces, the quiet that surrounds me, and the feeling of freedom that fills my soul. I inhale deeply, and bow in gratitude feeling the coolness of the earth beneath my bare feet.

I am starting to feel connected to the bigger picture of life just like in the vision.

Lou

Chapter 14

Growing Apart Together

Truth drives my passion to keep moving beyond, to welcome change, to learn, evolve, grow, and to become One with the world I live in.

The relationship between Garry and me starts to change over the years.

He is a homebody. I am a traveler and adventurer. He is used to, and comfortable with, routine, predictability, and habitual practices. I live with and thrive on, spontaneity, change, and new adventures. I want to color outside the lines and Garry needs to stay within the lines. There are times when our differences work to our advantage. We balance each other's energies or invite one another to push past our comfort zones, but there are times when it does the opposite, and over the years, except for our four children, the differences start to outnumber what we share.

We never fight. We discuss, we disagree, we leave the conversation in a huff and bang the door, but we never scream, call each other names, swear (at least not out loud or to each other), nor is there ever any physical shoving or pushing around. The denial and silence we both fall into is more insidious, damaging, and soul sucking than screaming matches or throwing things at each other can be. The refusal to acknowledge what's happening and the resistance to change starts to create wounds that carve craters in the essence of who I am.

Over the years, we often try to talk things out, and twice we seek help from professionals to try and better our relationship, but changes are slight and temporary and it doesn't take long before everything slides to the wayside and we are back to our distant and separate selves once more. To the outsider, except for us not doing much together, I'm sure everything looks fine, but on the inside, the distance between us widens like two cars travelling in opposite directions.

In the first years we share more as a couple and family, but as time goes on, there is less and less of that happening. For the most part that means I quit trying to cajole, convince, or bribe Garry into doing things or going places. I quit waiting for him to make plans, and instead start making my own plans for the kids and me, tell him about it, and extend the invitation for him to join us.

Through all of that, I don't believe either one of us ever intend to harm or hurt the other. We are just two individuals who in their own way are fighting to be true to who we are, and in our struggle to do so, somehow we grow further apart instead of getting closer together. That's not to say there aren't any good times in our twenty-three years together. There certainly are, and those moments along with a fundamental friendship and a respect for each other is what allow us to stay together for as long as we do.

When work requires I go take some training courses, and my time at home is limited, or when I am working at the office or teaching courses in the community, Garry takes charge at home and does what needs to be done. When it comes time to do the farm work, I am there to work with him on the trucks, tractors, and whatever else needs to be done around the farm or in the fields.

Then the unthinkable happens.

Dear One:

That feeling of connection and of "being one with" that I talked to you about—I want more of that. I don't think it's possible to live that every day in every way but I know it's possible to live it some days in some ways.

I try to explain it but how does one explain the invisible, the untouchable—something rooted at a deeper level than the everyday surface level of life?

Our relationship often lingers dangerously close to empty. We limp in a hollow existence from one day to the next. How do I manage to hang on to life when we live that way?

Lou

Chapter 15

The Unthinkable

Help me see the light in the dark.

November 21, 1984, my husband Garry, my mother-in-law, my son Kevin, and my three daughters, Karen, Jody, and Brenda gather around the kitchen table to celebrate Garry's thirty-third birthday. Garry blows out the candles, cuts the cake, puts a piece on the dessert plates and passes pieces around to everyone. Kevin as usual is cracking jokes.

"What do you call a crate of ducks?"

"What?" Karen asks.

"A box of quackers!"

"What do you get if you cross a chicken with a bell?"

This time Jody jumps in. "What?"

"A bird that has to wring its own neck!"

Everyone is laughing, but Kevin, who always enjoys his own jokes, is the one who laughs the loudest. He reminds me of Red Skeleton who could never keep a straight face or hold back his own laughter when getting to a punch line.

In the middle of the commotion at the kitchen table, I try to review a "to-do" list with the children as well as a few last minute instructions for my mother-in-law. She will be taking care of the kids while Garry and I make our way to Kelowna to a forty-fifth wedding anniversary celebration planned for my mom and dad.

"Kevin, make sure you take out the garbage every day and keep the downstairs clean. Karen, your job is to make sure the dogs and cats are fed, and help with setting the table and cleaning up after supper. Jody and Brenda, your job is to empty the dishwasher, pick up your toys and keep your room clean."

Everyone reassures me they know what they have to do and not to worry. We are leaving the next morning right after the kids get on the bus and head out to school. Six of us are travelling together, my sister and her husband, my brother and his wife, and us. We are traveling through the Rocky Mountains in the middle of winter. Today we keep going past the halfway point of Valemount and make it to Kamloops before stopping for the night.

In the morning, we take our time and enjoy a leisurely breakfast together before leaving for the last leg of our trip. The surprise celebration is to take place at my sister Danielle's place a few miles outside of Kelowna.

A couple of hours later, we pull into my sister's driveway. I am the first one to jump out of the car and walk up the steps to their house. I am about to knock on the door and shout, "We're here!" when the door flies open. Danielle takes a quick look at me, and just as quickly looks past me at the others who are making their way up the steps. Danielle's eyes look kind of funny. I get that queasy feeling in the pit of my stomach again. Something isn't right.

I am expecting her to say something like, "You guys are here already!" Instead, her eyes get even redder than they were when I first looked at her, and the look on her face is as if someone caught her in the middle of doing something she isn't supposed to do. "Where have you guys been? I've been trying to reach you for hours." There's a panicky edge to her voice that makes my stomach muscles contract and squeeze the air out of my lungs.

My mind races. Maybe something happened to Mom or maybe it's Dad. Most likely Dad. Maybe he had another heart attack. Maybe he died.

"What's the matter?" I ask. Danielle turns in my direction and when our eyes meet, my heart skips a beat or two like when I step into an elevator that takes off too quickly. "Lou, something's happened. There's been an accident. At home. It's Kevin."

"An accident? When? Last night? A snowmobile accident?"

It was the only way he could have been in an accident. He didn't drive. He wasn't going anywhere. "What happened? How bad is he?"

"No. No." Danielle says. "He wasn't on the snowmobile. He was at home. He got sick. The ambulance came for him. They flew him to Edmonton. Lou, it's bad. They don't know if he's going to make it."

I stand frozen in the same spot on my sister's deck. Inside me, my stomach lurches. The elevator drops and crashes to the bottom floor. I can't move. I can't breathe. My chest caves in. I try to form words, but no words come out. It is painful to swallow and hard to remember how. My ears throb. The echo of voices around me become muffled but loud, like they are on the other side of the elevator doors. Close, but far way in the distance, the pounding in the back of my head is sharp, painful. Deafening. More words jar me out of the fog. "Booked you a flight to Edmonton. You have to leave right away. Drive you to the airport. Here's your tickets. Carmen will meet you, bring you to the hospital. Get in my car.

We have to leave right away. You'll miss your flight. There isn't much time. Hurry!"

Someone digs our bags out of our car and throws them into Danielle's SUV. She hands Garry two tickets for a flight to Edmonton via Calgary.

"It's the only flight I could get you on. It leaves in half an hour. I can get you to the airport in ten minutes. Let's go!"

The ride to the airport, checking our bags, going through security, boarding the plane, all of it feels like an out-of-body experience. I am vaguely aware of Danielle talking about the calls she received, about Kevin being on life support, about how I will find out more once I get to Edmonton. Garry is there. He buckles my seat belt, picks up the suitcase, hands me Kleenex, tells me where the bathroom is, which way to turn to board the plane, where my seat is. I follow like some kind of malfunctioning robot, my heart working hard to pump blood to my wooden extremities.

I question Garry to see if we're on the wrong flight. It's usually a fifty-five-minute ride to Calgary and a twenty-minute ride to Edmonton. What's taking so long? Why aren't we there yet? We must be on the wrong flight. Garry reassures me we're not.

"We're about to land in Calgary," he says.

He's right. I hear the pilot announce our descent. I close my eyes and pray the stop will be brief.

People shuffle back and forth. Some deplane and others file in to fill their empty seats. They are moving in slow motion and I silently curse each one for the precious minutes they are wasting trying to stuff their over-sized bags in the overhead compartments. I want to scream at them, but I can't find my voice and I say nothing. I stare into the distance, and the voice inside me repeats the same thing over and over again, and I pray the message will somehow reach Kevin telepathically.

"We're on our way, Kevin. Hang on, you hear me. You have to hang on."

At last passengers are settled. The hatch is closed, the plane is de-iced, and we speed down the runway heading to the Edmonton International Airport where Carmen will pick us up.

Dear One:

I am on my way to see Kevin and be with him.
Once we're together, everything will be okay.
Lou

Chapter 16

The Quiet Room

Our greatest alignments with truth often come through our most difficult life moments.

Carmen, Garry and I bolt from the car and run through the hospital maze to the floor where I am told Kevin is. Carmen works here and knows the layout of this cold looking aseptic University of Alberta Hospital. She leads us to the doors we're to go through. "This is where he is," she says.

I raise my hands in front of me and move forward pushing against one of the double doors. It doesn't move. I try the door to the left. It doesn't move either. I panic. I back up a few steps turn sideways and rush forward giving the doors a shoulder check with enough force packed behind it to knock an NFL linebacker to the ground. Nothing. The doors don't budge. They are electronically locked. I notice a little window at the top of each door. It's heavy glass with a meshing inside. It reminds me of a prison. I stare at the door with enough intensity to bore a hole through it. Somewhere behind those doors, my son is being held hostage.

Then Garry notices the sign, "No Admittance Unless Authorized." There's a button underneath it that says, "Ring for Assistance." I push the button. A voice comes on over the intercom above me. "Your name please?" I wonder which name to use, Lou or Annette. Instead, I say, "You have my son Kevin. He was flown in by air ambulance. I'm his mother." The doors open immediately. A nurse comes out and puts her hand on my arm. "We've been waiting for you to arrive," she says as she leads Garry and me through the doors.

"Where is he? Is he okay? I need to see him. Where is he?"

"He's in the next room. Follow me. I'll take you to him right away. You have to be prepared though. He's on a respirator. He can't breathe on his own. You go on in and I'll get the doctor to come and talk to you right away." With that, she opens the door to the room where Kevin is, and as she walks away, I walk in.

What is a mother to do when a child full of mischief, words, and laughter falls silent? What is she to do with the battle of opposites that rips her insides? I look at Kevin lying in the hospital bed, naked except for a starchy white sheet. His arms extend on each side of him and rest on top the sheet. His eyes are closed and except for his skin looking more pale than usual and the ventilator pipe tucked between his lips, he looks like he is sleeping. I watch his chest rise and fall with the rhythm of the respirator. I pass my hand through his hair, take his hand in mine and watch for a sign, a flicker, something, anything that indicates life. None comes. I am surprised. I fully expect some kind of reaction. Doesn't he know I am here? Then I get mad. I want to say, "Okay, Kevin. you've carried this prank far enough. This isn't funny anymore. It never was. Now, wake up. Wake up!"

I zero in on his eyelids and the curve of his lips over the respirator. I expect him to blink then bust into a huge grin and crack up laughing like he always does with his sisters. Then as proud as ever saying, "Ha, ha, I got you. I got you good!"

But he doesn't move. He doesn't twitch a muscle or bat an eye. He just lies there. Silent. Still. Solemn looking. My heart starts aching as if squeezed out of my rib cage. I try to swallow but I don't remember how. Something in me, the promise of what can be, sinks into a pit of darkness and despair. I move closer to him. Lay my head on his shoulder, stroke his arm, his face, his hair. "Kevin, Kevin. I'm here. I love you Kevin. Do you hear me? I love you. I love you."

I feel someone cup my elbow in his or her hand and whisper, "I'm so sorry." I turn around to see a man in green hospital scrubs. "I'm Doctor Harrison," he says.

"What's wrong with him," I ask. "What's wrong with my son?"

"Why don't both of you come into the Quiet Room," he says. "I'll explain to you what has happened and what's going on."

My thoughts drift to my son lying under a white hospital sheet, motionless, expressionless, as if he has entered his own private quiet room, while this doctor, a stranger to me, has brought me to this one. I sit across from this man in green scrubs and watch his lips form words that make absolutely no sense to me. Words that sound like echoes coming from the end of a long deep tunnel I am falling into. Words like, "aneurysm, ruptures, brain dead, keeping Kevin on respirators until you arrived, hoping you would consider organ donations." Esoteric words that rip me open, gutting me one piece at a time. The absence of life, I discover, is deafening to my ears. Then I hear that strange voice again scream from somewhere deep inside No! No! No!

As if to save me from the intensity of the present moment, my mind intercepts with questions. What is the real purpose of a Quiet

Room? What or who are they designed for? Are they to give those who enter a quiet space to receive devastating news, or are they to ensure a quiet space for those on the other side, so they don't get affected by screams that go on inside?

Then my mind snaps back to the present moment, to the here and now. "How much time?" I ask.

I am told there is very little time. Decisions have to be made now. Not to save my son's life. There is nothing they can do for him. The question is will the end of his life save someone else's. Am I willing to donate some of his organs to give someone else the life my son can no longer have? I look at Garry and he already knows what my question is and says, "It's your decision and I will support you with whatever you decide."

It is clear I'm the one who is going to make this decision. I want to tell the doctor, "Take my organs and leave my son alone." But I know he can't, and I know that's not what he's asking, and I know I am facing the hardest decision I've ever had to make in my life, and I also know it's a no-brainer. If my son's life or lack thereof can give life to another, how can I refuse? First, I have to find a way to form the words that feel impossible to say.

I take the form from the doctor's hands, go down the list of items like it's some kind of shopping list and I check the little box beside kidneys and eyes and sign the name Annette on the dotted line.

Then I wait. I wait on the sidelines. I've asked to receive confirmation of when the surgeries are over. I want to know for sure that others have received life. There's a part of me that I tell no one about. I want my son to receive life too. It's only when I get the news that, yes indeed, the surgeries have been successful and that Kevin's body has been moved to the morgue for an autopsy, that I give up on my secret hope. Kevin's life is over. I buckle at the knees like a paper doll and wail. A half hour later, I walk out of the hospital, leaving the spirit of my boy behind.

Note: My decision to donate Kevin's organs that day gave sight to a three year-old and a twenty-one year-old and his kidneys saved two more people from being hooked to dialysis machines for the rest of their lives.

What the fuck was that about?
Why take a fourteen year old? Why take my son?
Why?
What did he ever do to anyone?
I'll tell you what! Nothing! Not a damn thing!
Dear One? Oneness?
How can there be Oneness when people you love are ripped from your life? What role does Oneness play when people's hearts are ripped out of their chest?
Go to hell!
Lou

Chapter 17

Returning Home

Truth can hurt.

"**D**on't cry," Mom says. "Don't cry."

Mom is pacing back and forth by the kitchen counter at my house as if it's a short runway she's trying to take off from. She is puffing on her second cigarette since she got here ten minutes ago. Her, my brother and his wife, and my sister and her husband, have just arrived from Kelowna. I haven't stopped crying. I know that emotions, her own, or other peoples' make her squirm like worms in a frying pan, but I can't believe she's saying don't cry. What else am I supposed to do? Laugh?

"But, Mom," I say, "my son is gone. He's dead Mom. He's dead."

Her hands shake and her coffee comes dangerously close to the edge as she brings the cup to her mouth. Her whole body seems chilled to the bone even though it's seventy-two in the house. I know she is hurting too, and I wish I could reach out and hold her, comfort her, help her wipe the tears she can't shed, or somehow stop the flow of mine, but I can't. I can't tell her how much I love her or that it's what I wish she could do for me now.

Both of us are frozen by years of pushing truth and pain into a backroom and shutting the door. I can't give her what she wants this time. I can't hold back the fresh batch of tears that are making their way to the surface and threatening to erupt unannounced. My body no longer allows me to deny "what is." Asking me to deny something that rocks my whole foundation as a human being is like asking me to hold my head underwater and breathe.

She doesn't ask with words, but I can tell. I am a pro at reading her body language. I can tell by the way she looks at me, by the way her hands start shaking, or how she tries to make herself busy by wiping the table or the counter top for the fifth or sixth time, and by how she looks away when people start to cry. She wants me to steer things away from the immediate and the realness of the situation. She wants me to put on a brave face. Pretend and do the "right" thing.

She wants me to greet people at the door, smile, thank them for the food they bring, ask them how things are going, talk about the weather, say something nice about what they are wearing, the price of grain, or politics, or ask about their plans for tomorrow, next week, or next year—anything to steer the conversation away from the here and now, and the intensity of feelings that float around the house and permeate the air.

Mom's wishes conflict with mine.

I look her straight in the eye for as long as she allows my eyes to meet hers. My inside voice is screaming, "Don't ask me to deny. Don't expect me to push away what I feel and to pretend I'm okay." Then the heavy silence hanging between us is broken by my outside voice that very firmly says, "Not this time, Mom. Not this time."

In that moment, with only those few simple spoken words, it is as if she knows, and I know, that this is the beginning of things being different between us. This is the beginning of me no longer allowing her fears of being in the moment, her fears of reality, her fears of emotions and living and speaking truth hold me back.

I turn and open the door to neighbors, family and friends as they arrive. I welcome their hugs, and I hug them back, and together we talk and we cry, and even though it's difficult for her, I can see Mom makes a huge effort to remain in the room. Only when the conversation gets gut-wrenching and painful does she get up to check on the coffee, pick up some dishes or quickly sweep the floor. In her own way, she does what she can to work through her grief, and to help me with mine. It isn't until the next day, before visitors arrive, that Mom's caring ways touch every part of my heart and I understand even more.

Mom asks, "Can I get Kevin's clothes ready? What do you want him to wear?"

A little while later, I stand where she can't see me and I watch her ironing the clothes she has just washed and dried. She does it so meticulously and with such love and care that I can feel the love radiating across the room to where I am. Then, I watch as she pulls a tissue from inside her sleeve, dabs her eyes and wipes her nose, and in that moment, I find myself choking back a fresh batch of tears. Once more, I get it. It is like all the chocolate cream and lemon meringue pies she made for me every time I went to visit her in Kelowna, or on special occasions like my birthday just because she knew they were my favorites, and just because she cared. Here, too, as she is lovingly getting Kevin's clothes ready for him, she loves and she cares, and she is doing the best she can by giving of who she is in the only way she knows how. She feels my presence, turns around and in that moment, our eyes meet.

Neither one of us says anything, but she knows and I know. There is lots of love there.

Yes, Mom is there, and she cares. Dad does not come. He drinks instead. And because of the choices he makes, my older sister, Danielle stays behind to keep an eye on him,

The reality however—is that regardless of whether one chooses to be part of it or not, life and death keep moving forward.

Before the service is to take place, six of Kevin's closest friends and snowmobile buddies ask me if they can form an honor guard when Kevin's casket is brought into the church. Knowing that would mean a lot to Kevin, I agree. I also ask Kevin's grade eight band teacher if he would consider playing my son's saxophone at the funeral.

Mr. Bridgestone plays The Eye of the Tiger, the song Kevin was practicing the day before he died. He follows this by another piece, his own dedication to Kevin. He is flooded with emotion and has to stop a few times in order to take a breath, gather his strength and carry on, but everyone feels the love that pours from his breath into his fingers on the keys of the sax as he so eloquently plays these two pieces.

At the end of the funeral, when it is time to close the casket and say goodbye, I remove one of my three wedding rings from my finger, place it in Kevin's top jacket pocket and whisper in his ear, "You can give it back to me when we meet and we are One again."

Dear One:
  I still don't understand.
  I doubt I ever will.
  Lou

Chapter 18

Inside Snapshots

My mind wanders, drifts, sails, crashes, like a kite with no string.

Snapshot—Of What Happened

On November 23rd, 1984, at 7:45 in the morning, Kevin's alarm clock rings. He opens his eyes, gets up, takes a few steps towards his closet to get his clothes and get dressed for school, and he collapses in a heap on the floor. Later that same night, my son, who has never been sick a day in his life, dies.

For weeks after Kevin's death, I experience nightmarish kind of dreams where I sit bolt upright in the middle of the night. Often they are of Kevin standing at the edge of my bed, shaking me awake saying, "Mom, I can't breathe. Mom, I can't see."

The mind does strange and powerful things when it doesn't have adequate time to adjust to sudden events of such magnitude. It finds ways to release fears one can't fathom, much less express at the time. It tries hard to search for answers for something that wasn't possible, like a mother's need to protect and love her child. It takes a long time for those dreams to subside.

Life and death, if one allows them to, has a way of dropping a million questions right smack in the middle of one's lap. For me, those questions are matched with a fierce need to understand. Some days I find myself experiencing a deep compassion, as I have never felt before, for the world and everyone I come in contact with, including myself. Some days I want to walk out the door and never come back. Other days I want to be as far away from people as I can possibly be. I want to find a place where I don't have to do, think, or feel a blessed thing.

About a month or so after Kevin dies, I get a phone call, and the woman at the other end of the line says, "I'm just calling to remind you it's time to bring Kevin back in for his eye exam to see if he needs to be fitted for new glasses. Would you like me to book that appointment for him now?"

I answer in a flat monotone voice. "No, that won't be necessary. I gave his eyes away." My words are met with a dead silence that matches the dead part of my heart. After some uncomfortable moments, the woman catches her breath and says, "Excuse me?"

"Kevin died. He's dead," I say. More silence follows. I hold the receiver to my ear as if whoever is swallowing hard at the other end will somehow offer a solution to my reality. "I'm so sorry," she says. And to that, I answer, "So am I. So am I."

SNAPSHOT—Growing Up

"I'm never going to know what it's like to make love to a girl."

I am sitting on the edge of his bed when he utters these words to me. My son is devastated. His school sweetheart told him she isn't ready to have a boyfriend and broke up with him earlier today.

I can feel his sadness and his pain. "Ahh, Kevin, don't say that. I know it feels like your whole world is falling apart right now but there will be lots of time for you to experience making love to a girl. You thought you'd be with this girl forever because she means so much to you, but you're only fourteen. When the time is right, and it's the right girl, things will come together for you."

I was wrong. Kevin was right. Two weeks later, my son is dead. He never gets to experience making love to a girl, and I wonder if in some inexplicable way, a part of him knew the unthinkable was near.

Snapshot—Back to Work

I'm trapped in a freeze frame, suspended in nothingness, a vacuum, caught between two worlds. The one I can't let go of and the one I'm being beckoned to step back into and don't want to.

I notice the clock on the wall above my desk is still ticking; the minute hand moves forward. My boss is on the phone making plans for a family celebration. He listens, laughs, communicates his excitement and anticipation, and sends his good cheer. I don't understand. How can everyone's world keep moving ahead as if nothing has happened, when mine has come to an abrupt end?

My co-worker Sherry gets a deposit ready for the bank. She adds cheques, and counts cash. Someone drops by the office with a complaint about their bill. All of it seems so trivial, so meaningless in the whole scheme of things. Who the fuck cares!

My stomach doesn't feel so good. I am nauseous and I fight the feeling that I'm going to be sick to my stomach with dry heaves. The sense of normalcy I'm witnessing as the world continues to go about its business is vexatious and denies my reality, yet at the same time, it is comforting in some strange way. It lets me know I am here, although I'm not sure I want to be.

I am expected to step back into the world, to go on as if nothing happened, to hang my grief on the coat rack by the door. But grief doesn't work that way. It has a mind of its own. I can't hang it by a belt loop, lock it in a vault or squish it into a ball and throw it away. It trickles out like water in my hand or sand between rocks. The stuff that grief is made of permeates into my pores. One minute I'm fine and the next minute it oozes out of me or explodes like someone hitting a gas line when digging in a backyard.

Coming back from work one day, I drive into the yard and sitting on the patio propped up on its kick stand is Kevin's two wheel bike I stored in the garage because I couldn't bear to look at it after he died.

My insides flip-flop and I hear myself say, "Yippee! Kevin is home!" I throw the car in park, reach for the door handle to jump out of the car and greet him, and in the next moment, the cold hard knock of reality takes my breath away.

The silence of death is deafening.

Snapshot—Reflections

At fourteen Kevin was just crossing over the threshold of childhood, a tall sometimes awkward teenager with several manly features sneaking their way in.

I call home from work one day and hear this deep manly voice at the other end of the line. "Who is this?" I ask, thinking I have either dialed the wrong number or there is a stranger in my house answering my phone. "Mom, it's me, Kevin," he says. Then when I come home after work, there he is playing with his sisters and acting as if he too is five or seven years old.

One day I am working outside and when I come back inside he is all excited to show me the new game he and his sisters are playing. Two of them crawl into a sleeping bag, put a pillow under their bum, zip up the bag, sit at the top of the basement stairs, and shove off as if they were launching down a water slide, laughing and screaming, "bump, bump, bump," all the way down to the bottom of the stairs and the concrete landing below.

He certainly adds his share to the chaos of him and Karen and the two young ones, all growing up in the same household together. He argues, he sulks, he teases and complains, but he is also quick to forgive and say I'm sorry.

Some days he loads one or all of his sisters, whoever is willing to follow him, in his red wagon, along with a few boards and some nails, and off they go to work on his tree house in the bush at the back of the house. Then other times, like when I knock at his bedroom door to kiss him goodnight, I hear him scurrying around, quickly shoving his girly magazines under his mattress before he opens the door. On any given day, I can find him sitting somewhere writing a science fiction story, drawing pencil sketches of make-believe worlds and favorite cartoon characters, practicing his guitar and saxophone, or being all lovey-dovey over the phone with a girl.

SNAPSHOT—How I Feel

My son is never coming home. The task of emptying his room, and his dresser, of returning his Christmas gift just in from Sears, of setting the table for five instead of six, and of putting up a tree to celebrate Christmas feels insurmountable. I am ripped open, my insides strewn about and exposed for everyone to see.

On a cold winter's night, it all becomes too much, and I pace up and down the house, wanting desperately to escape, to run, and just keep running until the pain stops, or I drop from sheer exhaustion.

I open the closet where we store our winter parkas and ski-doo suits and swing the doors open. How stupid of me to have wasted time cleaning this closet the week before. All those precious moments, among others, I could have spent with him before he died. Why didn't I know? Why wasn't I told his time was limited? I was his mother. I had a right to know. A mother should have a right to know!

I yank a one-piece snowsuit with yellow stripes along the sleeves off the hanger, a toque I don't recognize as one of our own, some black mitts, and a red and white scarf that looks like some kind of Canadian memorabilia. I bundle up as much as I can, walk out into the dark of the night, and after several attempts, I manage to start our old snowmobile. I open it full throttle and speed off into the -40 degree weather.

A bitter cold wind comes rushing at me, biting into exposed skin. It doesn't take long for my outside to feel as numb as my insides. Ice crystals cling to my eyebrows and eyelashes like hoarfrost on a tree. I can barely feel my fingers and hands gripping the handlebars. The spray from either side of the snowmobile covers me in snow.

I cross our quarter section of land, cross a side road and several ditches on to another field. I am halfway down the neighbor's field when the snowmobile starts to jerk, sputter and lurch forward a few more hundred yards, then coughs and dies. It is then, in the stillness of the night, that I hear a noise unlike any I have ever heard before or have ever heard since. Piercing, deafening, howling, eerie cries. They come at me from everywhere and nowhere. Deafening noises that make my skin crawl. I throw myself into the snow and try to cover my ears with the inside of my palms, but I cannot stop the cries or shut them out. They are coming from somewhere deep inside of me.

As I am lying in the snow, death, I think, would be the easier choice, but something—a little inexplicable morsel of my heart urges me to choose differently. At that crucial moment when all I want to do is to let go, I hear, "You are not alone." And the vision of the five-year-old comes flooding back to me.

SNAPSHOT—What Was Supposed to Be

I am invited to go, and I do. I want to be there, but I don't. I act cool, calm, and collected, and I try to appear excited, but inside my stomach turns, and I swallow hard.

I stall as long as I can before I enter the gym decorated with balloons, streamers and artistically drawn profiles of each student on the walls. I try to slide into a chair in the back row without being noticed, but some heads turn, whispers are exchanged, and more heads turn my way.

I smile politely and nod, while inside, part of me wants to glare back at them and tell them I have a right to be there, while another part of me wants the floor to open and swallow me whole. I am thankful when the lights dim and music starts. Then the door opens and twenty-eight students file in. Parents' faces beam with pride as their son or daughter walk by. The lump in my throat grows as I watch the students make their way around the room and sit in a semi-circle on the stage.

Then one of the students gets up and goes to the microphone. He calls each student to come forward, and he reads a commentary about their achievements and future goals. It is easy to tell which corner of the room the parents are sitting in by how much louder the clapping is in that area of the gym. I sit back and watch and listen, and envy.

After the students have stood, each in turn, the young man at the microphone is silent for a moment. Then he clears his throat and speaks once more. "There is one more student who needs to be mentioned and who we want to remember here tonight. His name is Kevin".

It is my son's turn, only my son isn't there to hear his name being called, to walk on stage. Kevin is dead. He died in November and this is June of the following school year—this is prom night for the friends he has gone to school with.

My heart drowns in a combination of tears and pride as I listen to what Kevin's fellow students and friends have to say in his memory. Then, one by one, each student takes a rose from a vase on the stage and brings it to their parents who are sitting in the audience as a way of saying thank you, I'm grateful, and I love you.

When each of them have had a turn, there is one rose left in the vase and that is when I see my daughter Karen walk up on stage, take the last rose from the vase, and with tears streaming down her cheeks, I watch as she makes her way towards me.

Somehow, I manage to get off my chair and make my legs move forward. If she has the courage to do this for her brother, then I have to find the courage to get up and meet her halfway.

Later, while preparations are made for the dance, I go talk to Kevin's closest buddies, and to their parents. I hear my outside voice speak of how lucky they are and how proud they look, and I swallow hard to muffle my inside voice filled with screams of jealousy. The voice that is shouting how it isn't fair, their sons are alive and well and they can leave knowing their son or their daughter will be coming home later but mine won't be.

My son isn't coming home. The front door won't open, and I can no longer watch him head to his room and hear him call back, "Good night, Mom. I love you." I have only memories.

Dear One:

People say it will get better, be easier, not so painful somehow. I'm not sure that this is true.

I'm not even sure I want it to get better or to hurt less—I'm scared that will mean he's slipping away from me even further than death has already taken him.

I know I'll never stop loving or missing him, but can I learn to live?

Lou

PART TWO

Chapter 19

The Turning Point

The mind goes over and over what the heart can't forget.

The death of a child often changes people. It changed me.

There's a mountain of grief, sitting on my chest. Every breath hurts. I am numbed by the pain. I drift from day to day floating on life's edge, and sometimes I want to disappear from life altogether. Yet, while part of me wants to curl up and die, another part of me refuses to be quieted. That part cries out to find the lost parts of me, and to be as engaged in life as a child with a sand box full of toys.

Blood continues to pump through my veins but a part of me has died. I try to pull myself out from under the blanket of grief which has descended upon me and my family, but by the end of the day I am exhausted. Depleted. Empty like a carved pumpkin after Halloween. The grief and pain threaten to be more than I can bear yet something within me struggles and fights to come alive.

I have to do something. Then one night just as suddenly and as clearly as a bolt of lightning flashing across a darkened sky, it hits me, and I know. I need to get help!

But reaching out for help because of how I feel is unheard of, shameful even. It's admitting I can't cope, can't do it on my own. I was brought up to be strong, not to cry, to figure things out for myself, and to make my own decisions. I am supposed to "take the bull by the horns," go for the full ride, and grin and bear whatever comes along. How can I possibly reach out to someone and say, "Help me, please, I can't do this on my own anymore?" Reaching out for help is like taking a leap off the edge of the cliff and plunging into the unknown. But the part of me that keeps refusing to be silenced tells me I can't just stand there. I have to take a leap. I have no other choice.

If life can be there one minute and gone the next, if without warning it can so abruptly be snatched away, then life, and the everyday living of it, has to be more meaningful and worthwhile than what I lived in the past and what I am living now. I want and need to live a full and meaningful life and in order to do that, I have to move through this pain.

What I don't know is that one thing touches another and that everything is intertwined like a great big bowl of spaghetti. And little do I know, that in order to touch joy, I have to touch sadness. And in order to touch love, I have to touch fear.

It takes me a long time to come to a place where I understand that I have to release what is, in order to start to make room for what can be, but I know that if I can somehow embrace this, I will find the strength to go on.

I begin to open my heart to the idea of my relationship with Kevin taking on another form, and I start to realize that life is a continuum, and just as a bend in the river doesn't mean that the river ceases to flow, the death of a person doesn't mean they cease to exist. I begin to understand that life doesn't just end, it transmutes, and that the dead do not really die, they live on in our hearts for as long as we want them to.

All the great spiritual teachers teach us that life is eternal and that death is but an illusion, a passing to another plane. Every day I try to remind myself of this and hold on to it as much as I can. I am a child learning to walk, and Kevin is the one holding my hand.

He is no longer part of my physical world, but the essence of who he was very much remains alive in me. Every day I talk to him or his spirit, or whatever it is that remains when a person is gone. Sometimes I sit at his grave site and ask him for the courage to keep celebrating life and the strength to live it authentically and connected to my heart.

What brings me comfort and keeps me going is the thought that in some ways, great or small, and for a period of time, however short it was, Kevin's life brought value to other people's lives and to mine. Something about this makes me want to jump into life with both feet and to be more immersed and present than I ever was before.

It's the beginning of that something that gives me the strength to get up the day my knees buckle beneath me, when I find myself in the middle of a field, face first in the snow at forty below. And it's that same something that whispers to my five-year-old self, that each one of us matter, that we are all unique, and that at some level we are all connected and in many ways we are the same. That's when I know.

I know that I not only want to—I have to be more fully engaged and present to life in order to live the closeness and connection that I see and live every time I connect with the vision of the five-year-old. I know that in order to get to that place, I need to first find myself and the words I swallowed a long time ago. I need to be closer to, and one with myself, others, and life itself.

I don't want to be someone who runs away from, shuts down, wears masks, or floats around in a sea of denial. I want to be someone who is transparent and real. I need to be filled with hope instead of despair. I need to believe in life instead of loss. I need to believe in transformation instead of death. I need to trust the rhythm of life, and flow with the constant changes it brings. I need to have Kevin's short life and what is obviously meant to be my longer life, have meaning and purpose, and in order to do that, I know I need to get through the pain, and I need to find my voice. Only then will I be able to be fully present, connected, and whole. As sure as I am that the sun will rise and set tomorrow, of this too, I am sure.

Now I have to figure out how to get there.

Dear One:

How do I get from the pain and the fear to the connection and the Oneness I know can exist?

I know we are connected, not just to the people who are currently in our lives, but to everyone and everything and even those who have gone before us. We are part of a universal dance and if we don't learn the steps to this dance we're going to find ourselves alone and lonely and we'll feel like we've been left behind.

Even if we think we're alone, we're not. We're part of a larger family, a system, a team. People have touched and shaped us. We have touched and shaped them. Each interaction creates a ripple effect. Each encounter helps shape our destiny.

The death of someone close has the power to transform us, or at the very least move us beyond who we pretend to be, or think we should be. It holds the power to awaken us to who we really are. It shifts how we see and view the world.

Death awakens us to life and how we want to live it. Kevin's death, as I see it now, is the impetus urging me to reach out for help, for life, and how I want and need to live it.

I hope to find the courage and strength to follow through.

Lou

Chapter 20

Reaching Out

Courage is walking down the road with my name on it even though there may be an easier path.

I don't remember where I get her name or how I hear that she helps people, but I remember thinking maybe, just maybe, she can help me find a way to relieve this unrelenting pain. It's my only hope. I have to try.

By the time I convince myself to pick up the phone and call Emily's number, I've worked myself into such a frenzy, that I'm shaking like someone plucked from a glacier fed lake.

How do I surmount thirty-three years of "don't talk" "be strong" conditioning? How do I reach out for help and feel okay about it? This is not at all the same as going to someone, saying our relationship is broken, and we need help. This is going to someone and saying, "I am broken and I need help." I chastise myself for even thinking about picking up the phone. How can I think someone can help me piece myself back together when a major piece of me is missing, and will never be here again. No matter how good she might be, she won't be able to bring my son back.

Still, I know I need help. I need to talk. I need to hear my voice say those ugly words out loud. I need to get the words, "Your son is dead, your son is dead," out of my head. The words keep coming over and over, louder and louder, like the piercing sound of an ambulance siren speeding towards me making me want to cover my ears. Merciless words that cannot and will not be silenced.

Maybe, just maybe, if I actually speak those words out loud, if I give them voice, maybe, just maybe, it will change something. Maybe it can silence the never-ending pounding force of those words in my ears, plug the hole in my heart or ease the bitter taste in my mouth.

I am rather incredulous about the whole idea of going to see someone, but even a tiny ray of hope, as slim as it might be is worth reaching out for. I decide to make the call.

It's impossible for me to realize then how the woman at the other end of the line will open her arms and heart to me like no one ever has. Little do I know of the unconditional love that awaits me on the other side of that door, the magnitude of how it will impact me, and how a woman by the name of Emily will play an instrumental part in the next leg of my journey.

When the day of my appointment arrives, I timorously make my way up the stairs to her second floor office. My legs are lead heavy, my heart pounds against my chest wall, and my skin is damp with perspiration even though it's freezing cold outside. I raise my hand and knock meekly at her door. I have already decided that I will only knock once. If there is no answer after the first knock, I will take it as a sign that it isn't meant to be, and I will head back where I came from.

She knows. Not of the intensity of the fear that sits in my gut and makes it feel like it's on fire, but she knows how important an immediate response is the first time a client comes to her door. The door opens before I sink further into the well of fear and have a chance to think about putting plan B into action.

"Hello, come in, come in," she says with a warm welcoming smile. "Come and sit down."

I step over the threshold as tentatively as a child just learning how to be steady on its feet. My eyes quickly survey my surroundings as I look for a clear escape route. I choose a chair where I can keep the door in full view. Emily sits in a chair kitty-corner to me and looks at me expectantly.

I swallow hard. My tongue feels heavy, clumsy, like it's too thick for my mouth and there isn't enough spit to allow it to slide into its proper place. My eyes dart around the room searching for something to focus on as I desperately search for my words.

"I don't know what to say. I don't know where to start," I manage to whisper.

There is a moment of silence where I risk stealing a quick glance in her direction without looking her in the eye. Her face is kind. She looks contemplative as if she knows she needs to proceed gently. I like the fact that there's a pause between her words and mine. When she speaks, her voice is tender, warm, receiving.

"I understand. It's very difficult, isn't it? Listen, Annette, start wherever you want. It's not important at all where you start. You can start anywhere."

Something about those simple words, the way she says them, and her strong presence, manages to sneak under the protective wall I've erected around my heart over the years. I let my eyes briefly scan the room. The sun is streaming in through the two big windows on either side of where we are sitting. There are several plants, one hanging from the ceiling, one on her desk, and one on a bookshelf full of books. I catch a glimpse of a book by Louise Hay called, *You Can Heal Your Life*, and another one by Thomas Harris called, *I'm Okay, You're Okay*, which strikes me as ironic, but that's all I have time to take in before I look down again. I'm trying to conceal my cold, sweaty hands and fingers that continuously cross and uncross like a weaving machine. I wipe the inside of my hands on my pant legs, but it doesn't take long they are all sweaty again.

I hope the words will come, but they are wedged inside me like a logjam at the mouth of a river. Emily waits patiently. Never prying or urging, just being with me, ready to receive. There is no pressure coming from her, but I can feel my own self-imposed pressure, which is more than I can bear. I have not yet uttered a word about why I am here or why I have come to see her. My anxiety level is dangerously high. A wrong word, or a wrong move will have me running for the hills and Emily senses it. She silently sends me loving energy and waits patiently.

Inside my head, a battle of the voices rages. One urges me to leave and run as fast as my feet can carry me, the other urges me to stay put and calm down. "Get out! Run! Say something. No. Don't. What can you say? She can't do anything for you. Don't be stupid. But this is your only chance. It's do-or-die."

Then I hear her voice again and it is like a soothing balm to a third degree burn. "It's so difficult, isn't it? So, so difficult for you," she says.

A tear runs down either side of my cheeks, my lips tremble and the words, "My son is dead," drop out of my mouth and hang in the silence like an off-key note at a piano recital.

Dear One:

Okay, I'm breaking all the rules by speaking up. Or at least that's the way it feels. But who cares—I wasn't the first one to break the rules was I? Children aren't meant to die before their parents. It's not the right order of things!

It's hard for me to get it—why an innocent young boy's life would be taken away. There's no sense in that. None!

Now that I've reached out for help, part of me feels a little more anchored. Knowing there is someone I can talk to helps. Even if I haven't been able to say much of anything just knowing someone is there is reassuring. At the same time I'm scared shitless.

But I know I have to do something. I have to keep reaching out. I can't just drift downstream like an uprooted tree. I have to reconnect with the purpose and meaning of life. I have to find a way to keep it together and be there for my girls. I have no choice.

Lou

Chapter 21

A Safe Place

Most people express themselves without difficulty. I just limp along.

As we approach the end of my session, almost all of which has been in complete silence, I am sure she will never want to see me again. How can she help someone who can't talk, and whose only words so far have been, "My son is dead."

At the close of the hour, she is still at my side sitting with me in my pain. Her total and complete presence is so real. It's almost like I can reach out and touch it. It boggles my mind. Most people need to break away from silence because it makes them uncomfortable. Emily doesn't need to fill the void with her words. She is comfortable to just sit with me. She holds the space where my pain lives and waits patiently to receive my words when they are ready to be shared.

As our hour together comes to an end, Emily tells me she would like to explain what her method of working with people is, and lets me know that if this is okay with me, she will be happy to continue to see me. I am interested in her method and want to learn more, but I am completely taken aback by her willingness to keep seeing me. My mind conjured thoughts that she would never want to see me again and would find a polite way of letting me know, but when she walks me to the door she says, "I'm glad you came to see me, and I'm ready to help you. Think about it, and let me know if you'd like to come back."

"Thank-you. I will let you know," I respond as I quickly make my way back to my car and leave her standing at the door watching me drive away.

The smaller more confined space of my car acts as a safe container, feels comforting and makes me feel more secure compared to the big wide open space of Emily's office where I felt so vulnerable and lost. I take a deep breath, and when I exhale, my breath makes a shaky raspy sound. A flood of anxiety washes over me. I feel like I am breaking all the rules, the ones that say, "don't see, don't touch, don't speak, don't feel," and I am filled with the fear of doing wrong and being judged. What can Emily possibly be thinking of me, a grown woman unable to speak.

I know I can't go home right away. I need time to assimilate what has just happened, and to figure out what has been touched in me as a result of the time I spent in Emily's presence. What are these strange new feelings that are floating around within me? I need time to sit with this.

In a desperate attempt to try to figure things out, I turn to what is most familiar to me, what helps me think things through and regain some sense of control. I turn the car in the opposite direction from home and drive and drive, and drive.

Being in the driver's seat, I'm sure is just an illusion of being in control, but for now, it's all I have, and hanging on to the illusion seems to help. The car offers me a private place to feel what I have to feel and to try to think things through.

Within this container, I can give myself permission to cry, scream, swear, and crack open the door to the fears I hold. All things I don't allow myself anywhere else but the safety of my car. Even though my exterior shows a "got-it-together" kind of disposition, I am like a minefield that is about to explode. When my eyes blur with tears or I am overcome with emotions and I get too shaky to drive, I stop on the side of the road or find an entrance to pull into.

My car becomes my safe haven and sometimes even my home away from home—a place where I can temporarily step out of having to cope with all the demands, and the painful reality of life without my son. Somewhere, somehow, I have to find a way to make sense of life, and what life has presented me with. Alone, cocooned within the boundaries of my car, no matter how ugly it might look I can allow my pain to be what it is, without the fear of being judged or of upsetting others.

In those moments of intense pain where I feel as if my heart has broken open, I start to see the world through different colored glasses. In the brokenness, I reach a more awakened state of being, and when I open my eyes and really look around, I find myself totally captivated by the beauty of what is before me. It can come through something as simple as a sunset I get lost in, the leaves turning colors on the trees, the sun rays that pierce through the dust in a farmer's field in a kaleidoscope of colors, or the Northern lights that dance in the night sky. It's in those moments, when I drink in the beauty of the landscape and the countryside that I start to get a glimpse of the concept that no one is meant to exist in a vacuum, that we are meant to be *One* with the bigger picture of life, and that somehow we are all connected with everyone and everything. Over and over again, the vision of the five-year-old that refuses to let go of me keeps bringing this truth home to me.

I want to trust this vision. I want to believe it can yank me out from behind the concrete wall I have constructed around myself, and the illusion of safety it gives me.

What I know for sure is that ever since my first session with Emily, a whiff of freedom and hope has followed me around everywhere. The woman's compassion and empathy has trickled its way into my heart and seeped into my veins like water poured over a mound of sand, and what I know for sure is, that no matter how difficult it is, I need to see her again.

I need someone to sit beside me and bear witness to my experience. I need to let go of my ingrained "don't talk, don't touch, don't feel, don't speak" rules that have cut off my voice and choked the words out of me. I need to break through the isolation and the old thought patterns of long ago that tell me I am on my own. I need to have someone understand and hear the words I cannot speak. I need someone to see me and hear me, and in many ways, I feel Emily already has.

Dear One:

Something happened when I went to see Emily. I don't know what that something is. I can only say that as uncomfortable and as difficult as it was for me to be there, it felt as if there was hope—like I was being rescued from floating away in the middle of the Arctic Sea on a piece of ice.

For that I can only say thank you.

I'm petrified but I understand what I have to do—what I need now is to somehow find the strength to carry through.

Lou

Chapter 22

The Call

I am not alone – but I alone can do this.

The next morning, I picked up the phone again.

"Hello," she says.

"I will come back," I tell her.

"Good, good. I'm glad to hear that," she responds. "I am able to see you on Monday at 4. Will that work for you?"

"Yes. I'll be there."

I enter Emily's office, sit with her in her space, and any words I might have had disappear like a puff of smoke in a gusty wind.

Again and again, week after week, I try to push words out of me, but it's like trying to push mud up a hill. I get nowhere. I sit there. Stunned and silent and lost.

Then one day, after one of those long almost completely silent visits, out of sheer desperation of not knowing what to do with me next, Emily hands me some sheets with a series of questions from a course on personal development and suggests I try to answer the questions through writing.

She doesn't know it yet, and neither do I, but she has thrown me a life preserver.

That same evening, after everyone has gone to bed, I grab one of Kevin's unused notebooks, curl up in my favorite chair, and I start to write. Before I know it, my pen has carved an imprint on my third finger, my hand is going numb, and minutes turn into hours as the moon rises and travels across the now darkened sky. And still, I write and I write, and I write. I have a focus now, a container that promises to hold the words I cannot speak, and the pain that short circuits my mind and leaves me feeling as if I've gone mad. I've pulled a string from a ball of wool and there is no way to stop the unraveling. There is so much I want and need to say. Writing down the words helps me fight the undertow that threatens to drown me. My pen serves as an anchor to a saner more grounded part of me. The busyness of my mind and the ache in my heart fall on the page and I continue to write until the wee hours of the morning while the rest of the world sleeps.

When it's time to go back and see her, I am shy and awkward about showing her my writing, but no matter how hard it is, I know I have to try. I can't give up on this. My stubborn determination makes me reach down into my backpack, pull out my notebook, and set it on the table in front of us. It sits there like a dead weight staring back at me, a traitor to a self-imposed vow of silence, evidence that I do have a voice hiding somewhere inside of me.

Emily waits for a while then asks me to read what I've written. Even if I had promised myself I would, the courage to do so slithers away. The words I have written glare back at me, daring me to speak them out loud, but I am silenced. My voice is gone. I cannot speak the words even if they are my own and I continue to sit there in the silence.

"Is it okay if I read your words out loud," Emily asks. I nod indicating, "Yes, yes, please do," and I let go of the breath I wasn't aware I was holding.

Emily reads my words slowly, attentively, comments here and there on what I've written, and then continues to read.

Every time I meet with Emily, she gives me more questions and more exercises to work with, and writing fast becomes a life raft I hang on to for dear life. It helps me to navigate the turbulent sea of feelings and emotions that live inside of me. I continue to write, and Emily continues to read, and after a while, I start to hear my voice come through hers, and the "*me*" of the moment slowly starts to emerge.

As she reads my words, I can see myself as a determined, funny, yet heartbroken adult—one who knows there is no choice but to keep moving forward and finish what I started with this therapy. Other times the only thing I see is a very frightened child, one who can no longer survive on her own now that she has allowed herself to be seen.

It takes a long time, but eventually, I am able to say a few words about me and explain how Kevin died. I still can't voice how I feel, but at least I can nod in agreement or disagreement to Emily's words.

Every week I book an appointment and every week I show up and inch forward in my healing and my growth. In some ways the hour, or more, I am with Emily feels as if it will never end and I can't wait to get out of there. In other ways, which I can't quite understand, her quiet and loving presence is so powerful that I don't ever want to leave. That's when I want to stay forever, suspended in this bubble of time where the struggle I go through, and the heaviness I feel, become lighter and a ray of hope sneaks in and warms me from the inside out.

It's as if Emily's love and compassionate caring lowers a ladder into my black hole of nonexistence, and her continuous encouragement and support helps carry me forward to a place of light and life.

When I feel I can't go on, she believes in me and gives me hope. When I feel discouraged and want to give up, she reminds me of the freedom I am seeking through my healing. When I feel I am going crazy, she normalizes things for me by explaining what is going on and why. She often adds, "It's coming, it's coming," to which I silently mutter to myself, "Sure, and so is Christmas," even if Christmas has just gone by.

And so, the weekly visits to Emily begin and lead to a process of transformation that takes shape over the next ten years. Her continual presence, her willingness to always be there, to always listen, receive, and most of all, to wait ever so patiently for my heart to open and for trust to build give me the courage to keep going back.

With her reassurance, I start to attack the limiting belief that keeps telling me that my words are not important. I keep coming back in the hopes that I can somehow transform into the person I know I am inside, and it's her unconditional love and acceptance that pulls me forward. For me it is the promise of fresh water as I make my way through parched desert land.

Still, no matter how enticing her continued presence is to my hungry spirit, I am not always a willing and eager participant. There are times when I can't see her often enough to satisfy my hunger, but there are also times when I plant my feet firmly in the ground and declare, "That's it! I've had enough. I'm done." And it takes days and sometimes weeks before I return.

But eventually I find my way back, and every time I come back, Emily receives me with open arms, and after a while, my walls continue to crumble and light seeps through.

Losing my son and the grief that followed is what brought me to her, but her unconditional love, understanding, and acceptance is what allows me to keep going and to dive into the deeper turbulent sea of emotions within me. As a result, my sometimes exhilarating, sometimes painful journey of self-discovery keeps moving forward and continues to unfold.

Dear One:

Well, I did it. I actually spoke a few words out loud. I read some of my writing to Emily. It wasn't much and it seems so trivial when I think about it. Yet it was so hard to do and if not for her unending patience and constant reassurance, I wouldn't have been able to.

All week I told myself that when I went to her I would not only read my writing to her but I would talk about it too. Then when she invited me to do so, facing that battle was like being thrown into a bullfighting ring with no legs to run and no place to go. What is wrong with me? Why is something so simple, so hard to do?

I'm a strong, capable, intelligent woman, I do well with anything I set my mind to do, I'm raising four children, (well three now), but this—this focusing on me, talking about me, figuring myself out and trying to live in line with this vision that follows me everywhere—that's damn hard to do and sometimes it feels like I'm chasing a cloud of dust. Can a person really live this Oneness? Is that maybe what scares me with the relationship that's developing with Emily?

Lou

Chapter 23

A Journal Sanctuary

It's funny how people scare me into silence and a blank page invites me to come forward and spill my words.

 T he suggestion that I try writing the words my voice cannot speak becomes as crucial to the survival of my soul as water, food, and shelter is to the survival of my physical being.

I try hard to move past the fear and let Emily know what I am living, but my words always get stuck and they are few and far between. Yet in my journal words drop off the end of my pen. My journal becomes my life line and I bring it with me everywhere. Whenever I get a few minutes, I pull it out and let my thoughts reveal themselves on the page.

April 04/85

People often don't have time, and sadly, often no desire or patience for someone like me, someone who needs to collect their thoughts so they can formulate them into words. People often can't afford to wait. The paper, it can wait. It's where I learn to trust my words and to trust myself. It's where I learn to bring my sensory experience into the world of words and action.

It's a huge struggle, more than anyone realizes, for me to externalize what I've internalized for so long. It's like trying to turn myself inside out or pulling at the moon. Words don't just automatically spill out of me like they do for most people.

It's a process that is beginning to happen in the safety of my journals, but I realize this is only the beginning.

If there's to be any hope of living the level of connection and Oneness I so desperately want to live in my relationships with people and the world around me, those feelings and words that find their way to the page will have to somehow find their way into spoken words.

Besides being a means of communicating what I'm living, my journal helps keep me grounded. I use it to ask questions, to analyze, to reflect, to understand, and to hear the whispers of my own voice that are barely audible even to myself. If for some reason I can't get to my journal for a while, I can sense how the most essential or the most precious parts of me can quickly start to recede, go underground, suffocate, and die.

My journal is my friend and writing becomes a meditative practice I use daily. It helps me break the silence, to learn, grow and have compassion for the woman who begins to emerge on the hundreds of pages I fill. I start to honor and respect this woman, and begin to understand that the learnings and the story behind the stories need to be honored and one day need to be told.

Dear One:

I fear. Fear the expression, the exposure, and the changes.

Tell me I'm not crazy when I think the words I'm writing will eventually lead to the connection and love I continue to see in the vision of the five-year-old that follows me, as consistently and persistently as the coming of the night follows the disappearance of the day.

How do I reconcile within myself the need to exercise my voice, to speak on paper, to see my truth appear before my eyes with the deeply ingrained belief that my words are not important?

How do I bring to life the depth of what I feel - the scene behind the scenes, the message behind the actions, the meaning within the spoken and the unspoken?

No matter how much I may curse, run from, or even try to ignore this incessant need to write, please don't let me give up. Don't let me lose my words no matter how vulnerable they may make me feel.

Without words, without voice, I will fail.

Lou

Chapter 24

Jumping In

I find truth in the silence, in the pause between the notes and in the space between my words.

Emily lessened my deeply held fears of not finding the *Oneness* I so desperately needed to find and feel.

Her focus is always to comfort, soothe, and help fill the huge crater within me. She holds me close and in the arms of love, the child within, the one who holds the truth of who I am, starts to emerge.

To have the needs of a child surface in my adult body humbles me, scares me, confuses me, and sometimes even frightens me. Emily reassures me that it's okay, and tells me to allow whatever comes to be there. "Just let go," she says. "Just let go." But letting go means allowing needs to bubble to the surface, and the huge struggle of letting someone see that I have needs feels insurmountable.

I am starting to think I have multiple personalities. One minute I am an adult in full control of adult thoughts and behaviors, and the next minute, I become a child with childlike needs, words, and actions.

The adult part of me understands that the opportunity to rescue this child and to integrate her within my adult self is a precious gift, but it's one I fight with constantly. I am scared to let her run wild and free. I fear she will get hurt again, yet I know it's in the moments when Annette fades into the background and Ti-Lou, in all her childlike glory, appears in the foreground, that are the most healing for me. This child is so real, genuine, spontaneous, and free, that I can't help but love her beauty and authenticity. Intellectually, I know that both of us, my adult self and my child self, must become one, but I'm not sure how to get there. I fear that the child will take over and I will no longer be the strong person I can be on the outside.

I see an image of my mom trying to hide her tears, and I feel my tears are not something I should let others see. I hear her voice say, "You're a big girl now, don't cry." And when my tears come, a ball of shame lodges itself in the back of my throat and makes it difficult for me to breathe.

I want to discover who I really am, not who I was shaped into being, and I know I will do what I have to do to get there. When I live as a mere shadow of who I am meant to be, it keeps me from "feeling the world" and I exist outside of it. I hang around the perimeters of my life and if I should dare venture closer to the center, I only dip my big toe in instead of bravely jumping in.

I don't want to do this anymore. I want to feel life—all of it. I want to immerse myself in the moment no matter what the moment is. I want to splash in the water puddles, chase after a balloon in the wind, drop on my belly and smell the first dandelion that pokes its nose out of the ground, run barefoot on the grass full of morning dew, and yes, I want someone to hold me and feel my tremors when I shake with fear, or feel the tears running down my cheeks if that is what the moment brings.

I am experienced, well versed, when it comes to the art of switching gears and setting things aside. Being able to separate myself at a moment's notice is something I have had to put into practice from the get go. It is something that was crucial to my survival as a child, but right now, it often works against me in my healing and my therapy.

I want to be like a sponge on a beach—my pores wide open to take it all in. Learning gives me a sense of moving forward, and more often than not, it is the most difficult moments that bring the most learning, meaning, and purpose to my life, so I throw myself into the learning, and like a dog with a rawhide bone, I won't let go.

Dear One:

Help me. I don't know what's going on. I feel like I'm two people living in one body. I don't have control over things the way I once did. It's as if I'm stuck between two worlds—an adult's and a child's, between needing to hang on and wanting to let go. I'm confused. Scared.

I'm writing and being asked to read what I wrote. It brings me back to my Dick and Jane first grade reading days. I sweat, I shake, and I shiver like a five-year-old. I'm barely able to get the words out even though they are my own.

I know love and kindness is waiting to receive my words. I know this intellectually, but the feeling part of me gets all confused with this. In my mind if I voice my words or read out loud it equals touching which then equals needing, which then equals loving—or have I got it all wrong? Does it really lead to love or does it lead to more abuse and shame?

I don't know if I should go back to see her. I want to, but I don't. It doesn't make sense. Why do I put myself through this? I don't understand. Why do I persist? What am I trying to find? What is it I'm searching for? Am I chasing after a vision that only exists within the context of my imagination or am I being drawn to persist with the work I've started with Emily because it offers a promise of truth, authenticity and the Oneness I search for?

Lou

Chapter 25

Healing Continues

Other people's truth is not mine to follow. I have to discover and follow my own.

Turning back, I realized, was not an option. Living life suspended in a state of limbo or by just going through the motions was not enough for me. I needed more to sink my teeth into.

I decide to continue to show up at Emily's door for regular appointments. I talk a little, but mostly about safe and unrelated things that have nothing to do with feelings. Anything to do with what is really going on inside, on a more personal or feeling level, I write it down. My journal becomes the place where I can speak.

Writing is the easy part. The next step proves to be more difficult. Before I go see Emily, I psych myself up to read from my journal, but when her invitation comes to do so, as it always does, I can feel my airways close like someone having an allergic reaction to a bee sting. My hands curl into fists, my body shakes and the words from the page get stuck in my throat like bugs in a spider's web.

And so it goes. Every time I see Emily, she invites me to read. And every time I try my hardest to do so. Then one day, through Emily's constant reassurance and loving presence, I make a breakthrough and am able to hold the images of my Dick and Jane reader at bay long enough to risk reading more than the few words I did before. Then I stop and wait to see what will happen.

Nothing bad happens. Instead, I hear Emily's voice encouraging me. "Good. Good. Go on. Take your time. You're safe here. You're doing well. Go on."

I read a few more words. I pause and wait. Again, I am encouraged to keep going. Gradually, the frightened little girl, within my adult self, dares to poke her head out of her shell and risk, and on it goes, until I risk a little more each day.

It is a slow and gradual process that takes place over months and years of hard work, but I am fueled by a sense of urgency to move forward and a stubborn determination to not give up until I reach the finish line.

I'm not sure how long it takes for me to speak without the use of my journal, but it is a long time, and not once does Emily show signs of giving up on me.

As I persist with my meetings and my work with Emily, a continuous internal battle rages on with both my adult and my childlike self, fighting for the upper hand. The transition back and forth from one state of being to another leaves me wondering if there is such a thing as "normal" and if there is, if I would be able to recognize it if I saw it.

My reflective self reaches for my journal and writes:

April 10/85

Within me, there is the hunger for deep unions, for meaningful relationships, for the caring, feeling and sharing of other people's hurts, pains and joys. I am capable of much more than this superficial above ground kind of life and I want a deeper more intimate one. I need to go underground and pull out the real me.— .the one who is waiting to be set free.

To do this I have to accept who and what I am now, and I trust the change will come. Being able to survive on my own, being independent and ignoring my needs has been my way of merely surviving, and it has served me well but I cannot do this anymore, nor do I want to.

I know I have to go back and figure out what I missed as a child and I will have to face my fear of rejection, hurt, and pain. I'm starting to realize there's no other way around it, but I often get impatient with therapy. I want answers from Emily. I want to know how long this process will take. I want to know how far away the finish line is, and what the completed puzzle will look like. There is no picture on the box to guide me. The pieces are scattered everywhere and I scramble to pick them up and make sense of them.

Emily, in her effort to encourage and inspire me, tells me over and over, "It's coming. It's coming." "What? What is coming?" I often demand to know. "What do you see? What does the picture look like?" I want a map for my journey. A compass. Specific instructions. Guide posts to indicate how much further. Rest spots with lemonade stands along the way would be nice, too.

But the only way others can help me is by building the framework for the journey I have set out on, and the rest is up to me. I'm the one that has to pick up each piece, turn it right side up, examine it, and figure out where it goes, or if it is even mine to keep. What I discover is that some pieces belong to my mother, my father, or the expectations of society. Those pieces don't fit in the image that is taking shape for me.

Dear One:

Here's what I think. What I need is devotion to truth. Most people, including me, live an assortment of lies. Because truth can be painful, we shy away from it instead of dealing with it and growing from it. In many family systems, truth is ignored, denied, or withheld, as it was in mine. Isn't that a little like trying to eat a banana without peeling it? How are we supposed to get to the good things inside?

It's like stuffing things in a closet until we have to lean against the door to clamp it shut. Sooner or later, we discover there's something in that closet we want, but we can't get to it without everything spilling at our feet. So, we keep the door shut. If we shut the door on pain, we also shut the door on joy. We can't separate or segregate feelings the way people prod and separate cattle.

Growing up in an environment where truths aren't spoken makes it hard to live from our core, which is where our beauty and our truth reside.

My truth is what I think and feel, but if my truth is never acknowledged, then neither am I.

That's how I feel. Unacknowledged. Disengaged. Dismissed. Denied.

Lou

Chapter 26

Opening Up

Breathe in faith. Breathe out action.

As my work with Emily progressed and I became stronger in my ability to express myself, my trust built, more things came forward in my writing and my journal was there to receive it.

May 6/86

I feel guilt, a lot of guilt. Maybe I'm the one who caused that teacher to molest me. Maybe it was my fault. It seems fairly clear now. I needed closeness and affection and I allowed him to give me some. What a dumb little kid I was.

I always thought that my parents didn't want to listen to me when I tried to tell them. I probably didn't try very hard, that's probably why. Maybe I loved the attention I got and didn't try hard enough to tell my parents. Maybe I didn't want it to stop. Maybe someone found out what was happening and made him go away. Maybe that's why he just disappeared one day never to be seen or to be heard of again.

I grew up pushing myself to be brave and strong and never wanted to need or depend on anyone's love and now here I am—trapped again, trapped in Emily's love and my growing need for it. I must survive without her love. I don't deserve it, and I can't allow myself to need her. I can't allow myself to be touched so deeply. I can't bear the thought of her disappearing, too, and all because of me. I wish she would just leave me alone. I can survive. I will survive. I've always survived.

The past few days I've felt like running. I want to run and run and run until I feel the physical pain—so much pain that I can't think of anything else. It's what I am doing in a way. I don't give myself a chance to breathe. I jump out of bed, and I'm off and running almost before my feet have a chance to hit the floor. I run around like a rabbit being chased by a coyote, and I don't quit until nighttime when I fall into bed exhausted.

I feel like hell inside and I try to put on a happy outside. I'm running because I'm scared of how I've become dependent on Emily. I can't allow myself to need or depend on her love and commitment like I do. I have to pull away from her.

I know it sounds crazy but I feel I have to protect myself. If I become too dependent, she might disappear just like my teacher did. I couldn't or wasn't strong enough to break away then, but I am now.

The strong need I feel to break away from Emily's love and caring, and my experience with Mr. Lebeau was all beginning to make sense to me now. Mr. Lebeau had scared me into silence, and it had become "our" secret—a secret that made me feel sick to my stomach. But in a strange sort of way, I felt something for this man, even if I knew that what was happening was wrong. In my five-year-old way of seeing and understanding things, I couldn't find a way to make it stop without hurting someone, so every time it happened, I slipped into another body glove. I kept quiet hoping nothing bad would happen. The guilt I carried was tremendous, and in no way did it belong to a child.

At least my teacher wasn't afraid of me. He was always gentle, always kind. He made me his ally, and I grew to like him in my own kind of way. Then one day he was gone, and I never heard from him again, and never found out what happened to him. Had I hurt him? Was it because he had been close to me? Was it my fault? Is that what happened to people when I cared for them or they tried to love me? They disappeared and I was left alone?

Now Emily is about to leave for an extended period, and here I am revisiting all this again, and I don't want to deal with it anymore. I don't want to deal with love coming and going, and disappearing. I want to feel pain, physical pain on the outside, so I won't feel the pain inside.

I hurt and I can't understand why. I am scared but I don't know of what. I want to get away, to run to the other side of the world—but run to what and from what? I don't know. All I know is love and hopes and dreams have a way of falling in mid-flight. All I know is that it hurts. Love hurts.

As my trust in the guidance I receive and the need to move forward grows, I go deeper into the healing. Sometimes the pen takes the words that have remained dormant inside of me, and brings those words to the surface, leaving them on the page for me to see.

July 24/87

I'm sorry. I'm really sorry. I didn't mean to let anyone love me. Honestly. I didn't mean to let this happen but he made me feel important. He listened to me and he made me feel like someone who mattered, not just someone that was in the way.

I knew I shouldn't feel good or let myself be loved because it wasn't right. I needed someone to talk to, to kiss me, to love me, to touch me, to understand me and I felt like there was no one there, as if I had to make it on my own. And you were so proud of me because I was so independent and strong, weren't you Mom? You never knew what was happening to me.

Did you? Did you?

I continue to write. Every day I write, and I write, and I write. Some of it I bring to session with me. Some of it I keep to myself. Writing is giving me a voice. A voice I feel I never had. It is still a silent voice, mind you, but a voice nevertheless and one that I feel will eventually help me emerge from within.

Over the years, Emily gives personal growth workshops and she always invites me to take part knowing I will likely benefit from attending. When she proposes this to me, my first thought is, "Absolutely not! No way in hell!" But the encouragement to take part and the reassurance that I will be okay keeps coming and at one point I decide to face the fear and attend. That's all I can promise and I am reassured that that is enough.

The experience petrifies me but also gives me hope. It is a taste of what I want more of in my life. Here, I find depth and meaning. I find people connecting and relating to each other from the heart. I see people grapple to discover their truth, dare to share it, and to have it received in a warm and supportive environment.

The whole experience blows me away. It is very close to what I have lived over and over again in my mind's eye as a five-year-old sitting at the window, and here I am witnessing an example of it right in front of my eyes.

The desire to be there, combined with the fear of being there are both as intense, one as the other. It's like a magnet drawing me in. At the same time, I want to push away from it and run as far away as I can.

I watch as people write and share what they have written, and when they share, I witness the healing that happens, and I think to myself, I don't know how, and I don't know when, but I too will offer this kind of experience to people one day.

Throughout the session, as I witness and hear others dare to share their personal discoveries about themselves, my own internal battle rages on. My insides scream to let me take part, and my fears tug at the reins and hold me back.

After the writing, Emily goes around the room and invites each one of us to share if we wish. Everyone does. Everyone but me that is. I remain: Silent. Mute. Paralyzed. Unable to speak even though I am dying inside to find my voice and connect to the people I am with.

On the last day of the course, I am feeling pressured, not only by a huge need to speak and make my voice heard, but also by the knowledge that the opportunity to do so will soon come to an end, so I muster all my courage and face my fear in the only way I know how.

While everyone goes for a coffee break, I stay in the session room, and I write a poem in my journal. Then, hurrying up before others come back, I write my poem on the board at the front of the room where everyone will see it when they return.

It is a whole new world
You have opened up for me.
Rewarding, interesting, puzzling
And scary, as you can see.

You ask, "Of what are you scared?"
And I wish I could respond
With a few simple words
That would illuminate the dawn.

This certainly is not something
I would have admitted to before.
So maybe just the realization
Should be considered as a score.

My well guarded independence
Has been rocked by great big waves,
Since I've met all of you and found
Relationships I've craved.

To have everything offered to me
That before was always denied,
Is something I have to adjust to
Before it can be surmised.

Having things out in the open
Can be quite an experience though.
I'm used to hiding everything
And that's probably what scares me so.

That is the closest I come to making my voice heard during the thirty hours of that workshop. As difficult as it is to take that session, and even though I can't get out of there fast enough when it is over, I know that one day, when the opportunity is there again,

I will be back for more. And I am. Four or five times more. The second session I take part in is more or less a repeat of the first time. I explore my inner landscape, I observe, I learn, and I write it all down, but every time I am invited to share, the fear consumes me, and no words come.

Again, it is only on the last day of the session that I manage to poke a hole through my concrete wall. This time when Emily looks my way to see if I want to share, I nod, yes. Just as quickly, I wish the floorboards to open so I can disappear or that I could just roll over and die. The air feels heavy with expectancy. I don't know if I can deliver, but I know I have to try.

I pick up my notebook to read my words but my eyes are moist and blurry, and my whole body shakes and rattles like when I am working the garden with the rototiller. I can't focus on the words on the page. I read three or four words and choke up. I hear a voice say, "It is okay. Take your time." I swallow hard, take a deep breath, place my journal on the stool at my feet, sit on my hands to control the shaking and slowly, like a grade one child, I start to read the words on my page. Only this time it is my page, my words, real words, coming straight from my heart.

Dear One:

I always acted like, and believed, I was strong, capable and untouchable. If something knocked me down, I bounced back right away. I didn't want to be seen as weak. I always felt I had to prove myself at anything and everything I did, and I pushed myself to do things no matter what the cost. I tried to make sure I didn't need anything from anyone else, or at least not to show it.

Now I need and depend on Emily to guide me on my journey and I don't know what to do about it. It drives me crazy.

I am disappointed with myself. What happened to the strong person I've portrayed myself to be? Have I lived a lie when it's always been so important for me to live in truth?

To ask for and to receive help is a lot harder than to give. I can't pretend. It just doesn't work for me anymore. My whole body screams for a deeper, fuller life. I am more than an empty vessel of shallow existence. I know that now. I also know that it's only when the real me is present that I feel alive. Can it be that some things need to be broken open before we can see the beauty inside?

It's humbling to admit I need help, that I want help, and that I can't do it alone. Maybe we're not meant to go at it alone in this world. Maybe we're not meant to exist in a vacuum. Maybe the vision I had as a five-year-old is the truth. Maybe that really is real life. Maybe we're meant to be connected to one another. Maybe we're meant to be One.

Lou

Chapter 27

Different World

Death has awakened me to life.

In the real world, the one separate from therapy, I was an adult functioning in an adult world.

I am a mother in a very busy household, a farmer working in the fields, a bookkeeper for an ambulance service, I have a job I go to everyday, and I participate in life and interact with people in a normal way. On the surface, I navigate the outside world as smoothly and efficiently as I can, but often at the expense of ignoring my inner world, which pleads for a chance to emerge. There is a growing restlessness to my spirit. Nothing seems to fit anymore and I search for a way to make things right. I find myself looking deep into people's eyes, trying to get a glimpse of what is going on in their soul, as if entering their world will somehow help me figure out or fill the hollow places I feel in mine.

On the outside, it looks as if things are back to normal since Kevin's death. On the inside I struggle to find answers to the questions that continually invade my mind like dandelions in a newly planted lawn.

Emily is the only one who knows what I am living. Many times, I try to involve Garry in what I am going through, but the more I try, the less he seems to want to hear. Perhaps our distancing begins because we deal with our grief each in our own way and we don't know how to be there for each other. Perhaps it's because I still struggle to find my words. Perhaps it is because Garry isn't interested in being a part of, or he doesn't know how to be a part of, sharing what we are going through. Whatever the reasons are, it's evident that Garry and I grow further and further apart after the loss of our son.

On numerous occasions, I try to discuss with him how I see the distance between us growing and how dangerously close we are to losing each other in the fog. Many times I bring up how I feel that the only thing we have in common is our children, and unless we work on our relationship, once they are gone, there won't be much left to hold us together as a couple. I tell him how important it is that we do something now to try to make things better.

To both our credit, we do try. Garry and I go for a total of five sessions with the marriage counsellor but at the end of these sessions the counsellor tells us that the gap between us is huge, and unless we are willing to meet halfway and walk together hand-in-hand there isn't much he can do to help us. Unfortunately, we never really find a way to meet in the middle. Garry is content to stay where he is, while I find I have to keep moving forward.

I am on a path of self-discovery, and although Garry never objects to anything that I choose to do, I think it scares him, and he wants no part of it, and to be honest, it isn't fair of me to expect him to want the same for himself. Maybe it isn't even fair to want him to be part of my process. He is quite happy with his life the way it is. I am the one who isn't happy or satisfied, living what feels to me like a superficial life. I want more depth, more meaning, and more truth. I want to sink my teeth into the nitty-gritty of life and taste every bit of it. So in a way, I move forward and he stays back, and the gap between us grows bigger and bigger as the days, months, and years go by.

Dear One:

I hope it is okay that I'm back again. There are things I need to say.

Except for raising my children, this life leaves me empty. I know it's what I've allowed myself to be molded into, but it's not me. Within me there is a hunger for deep unions, for meaningful relationships. I am capable of much more than the superficial life I live now.

Meaningful relationships, I realize can only happen by fully giving of myself, and I've tried, and I keep trying, to change this around in my marriage, but it goes nowhere. I work hard at expressing on the outside what I feel inside, but it falls on deaf ears. What is the point of feeling if I'm not able to share it with another or have another share feelings with me?

Even if we fear being vulnerable and even if we fear getting hurt in the process of being vulnerable, it is still worth the risk, isn't it? What we gain, and others gain, make it all worthwhile in the end, doesn't it?

If I don't live each day fully as who I am, if I never risk loving, then the pain will be even greater when death comes knocking at my door. Death makes us look at life, or lack of it. Death changes everything.

Why does it take something as big as death to wake us up to life?

The end, of life, as I've discovered, can happen anytime. As Kevin's sudden death proved to me.

Now I have a constant ache that sits in the hollow of my chest just beneath my breastbone that urges me to sit up and pay attention. It keeps telling me that I am meant to live life at a deeper level, do more and be more - that I need to find meaning and purpose in how I live and what I do.

What is that all about and what the hell do I do about it?

I know. I'm always asking questions, but the questions are yet another thing I've always kept inside. Not anymore. I'm done with that.

Now I will live the questions.

Lou

Chapter 28

Gaining Meaning

A life without changes is not a life for me.

A year after Kevin's death, I registered to take Crisis Line training in Peace River.

I get through the intense training, and although it is demanding and hard, I love every minute of it. After the training, I volunteer for over one hundred hours working on the line at night after my day's work at my regular job. This commitment requires that I travel an hour to the crisis center and an hour back home in the wee hours of the morning.

There are times, in the middle of winter, when I find myself white knuckling it on icy roads through blinding snowstorms or dense fog, but the sense of satisfaction I get after a night on the phone lines is the most rewarding work I have ever been part of. As difficult and as disheartening as some of those calls are, I leave with a heightened sense of purpose and meaning to my life. I am waking up to the piece of me that has for so long remained in the shadows.

I continue to work at my own personal growth with regular appointments with Emily and by attending thirty-hour self-development workshops being offered in the community. When I am unable to attend these courses in person, with Emily's guidance, I tackle the course work on a one-on-one basis with her. I love my work with the crisis line and the work I am doing to help further my own personal growth. I am finding a deep sense of purpose and meaning.

The experience of bringing my inner world to my outer experience is like a drug to me. I am on constant lookout to live life more authentically and I start to feel connected and invested in life on a much deeper level. When I interact with people, I actually see them, rather than just look at them. When I talk with my girls, I listen to try to understand and to grasp the feeling behind their words. When I write, I let the words stumble out of me, rather than guarding every word, or running circles around what I need to say.

The only place where I feel I fail miserably is with my relationship with Garry. Changes there are minimal. As much as I try to create change, it is like trying to make an anorexic gain weight. The small advancements in a positive direction never seem to stick around long enough to create any lasting change.

I start to look for some kind of employment or business that will bring more meaning and connection to my life.

Synchronicity, or what is meant to be, shows up the following week.

Dear One:

Oh my God! I applied for the job at Family and Community Support Services that was advertised in the paper. Have I gone mad? How would I do this job when I'm a work-in-progress myself? I definitely don't have all my shit together and it scares the willies out of me. There's a voice inside me saying, "Just who do you think you are?" Then there's another part of me that's telling me this job has my name on it, and it's time for me to step forward.

There's no doubt I've come a long way. I've learned, I've grown and I've changed. Man have I changed! I still have a ways to go, but I'm getting there and I'm ready for new challenges.

I need a purpose, a reason for being—a reason to get up and go to work in the morning. This job that just presented itself; oh my goodness, how I would love to do that! To work one on one with people as well as deliver social programs which are preventive in nature to promote and enhance well-being among individuals, families, and communities. It feels so right for me. It un-nerves me but I know, I just know, I can be good at it because my whole heart would be in it.

I'm in a much better place than before and I know my desire to help people doesn't come from a place of lack within me. It's not a crutch I need to help me walk. It's something I feel all the time. It's the solid part of me. The part I can rely on - the part that believes in the power of possibility and the importance of living a sense of connection and Oneness.

I gotta tell you, I'm nervous and restless as hell but I have to believe it's possible. I have to.

Lou

Chapter 29

The Power of Possibility

Shaping dreams into realities. That's what makes me get out of bed each morning.

In November, two years after Kevin's death, I landed the job at FCSS. I was on top of the moon.

My work is the best thing since mac and cheese. It nourishes me, gives meaning to my day and pulls out the best of who I am. It fills me with life but it also keeps me on my toes and makes me dig deeper than I ever have to dismantle the core belief that has shadowed me telling me my words are not important. I feel like I am living on a perpetual growing edge, constantly being pushed beyond my comfort zone, but I also feel alive and invested in something that has so much more meaning and purpose than spending my workday gathering checks, making deposits, and pushing a pencil around trying to balance accounts and ledgers.

I spend the next ten years at FCSS, and during this time, I develop some of the most meaningful relationships I have ever had. There are the two people who work the front desk Joce and Denise, the director Joyce, a co-worker Lil who works on programming with me and another program coordinator by the name of Aline.

Although the work Aline and I do is very different in scope, we often work together on various community projects, and I learn a lot from her. Aline is a born extrovert, a mover and shaker, a short, boisterous people-person with an infectious laugh, a kind, compassionate heart, a stubborn disposition, and a smile as bright as a sunflower that warms people's hearts when she greets them.

If Aline is moved, we don't have to guess. She lives her emotions out loud. Depending on the situation, she can get angry and explode like a firecracker, become emotional and tearful one minute, or exuberant with joy and rolling on the floor with laughter the next. Everything she is, I am not, and everything I am, she is not, and because of this, or in spite of this, we become each other's anchor, sounding board, and pillar of strength.

Through the years as I meet more people and get more known in the community, an even wider circle of friends become part of my world, and they eventually form my learning ground, my support system, and in many ways my family. With them and through them, I learn more about myself and what is of importance and value to me.

I learn to trust, open up, laugh, share, to care, to express myself more freely, and to be true to who I am. Like *The Elegant Gathering of White Snows* (Kris Radish), this circle of women prove to be just what I need to make some huge strides as I continue to move forward on my journey.

Then one day as I sit on the banks of the Smoky River with my journal in hand and reflect on how the water constantly changes, I realize I am living in the middle of deep meaningful relationships, the kind I have always yearned and craved for.

Mark Nepo, in *The Book of Awareness* states, "Too often, we can contain our way of being within our way of surviving." That's exactly what I have done in the past. My way of surviving has been to be like a turtle and withdraw within a protective shell. I know I can no longer live that way. Survival mode isn't good enough anymore. It suffocates me. Chokes me.

I don't want to just exist. I don't want to resign myself to "that's just the way it is." I want more. I want to live life all the way, and I vow to do whatever I have to do to get there. The Universe doesn't lose any time providing me with opportunities to step up to the plate and make it happen.

On one of those mornings when the sun is beaming through the two huge front windows at work and flooding the place with a warm radiant light, an old friend of the family who I haven't seen for years drops by. Danny starts to tell me about how he has studied to become a Life Skills Coach, and how he later trained to become a trainer of Life Skills Coaches. He explains how this intensive two-month experiential training is often grueling to get through, but well worth the expense, time and effort it requires. He goes on to explain how the eight to ten hours a day of class work is spent in groups where students acquire skills through experiential learning. This forces students to deal with personal issues that come to the surface and unless they do, they are not allowed to graduate from the course.

I listen to him describe how the program can create change for people and how it changed him, and I know I want this for myself. I want to have better skills to be confident in my work.

The words, "Send me the information, costs, program dates....I'm going to be there," spill out of my mouth before I have a chance to catch them. Just as quickly my inside voice screams at me, "Have you lost your bloody mind? What the hell are you doing?"

Just thinking about this training makes me break out into a sweat. Besides, it's crazy. A new job, three kids at home. I'm needed to help with the farming, I don't have the money, and the training is held in Edmonton, a five-hour drive from home. It's absurd, yet part of me doesn't doubt for a minute that, before long, I will be sitting in Danny's class.

I get to work making a proposal to the FCSS board asking for the training costs to be paid and for the time off. They agree. There's one condition. They want me to sign a paper promising that after my training, I will deliver a required number of workshop hours that will meet the FCSS mandate and benefit the community. I sign the paper.

Garry agrees to look after the children if the eight week training is when I am not needed to help with the farm work. I promise the kids that I will be coming home every weekend. Everything is arranged right down to my acceptance into the program for the following winter.

While I wait to go to Edmonton to take the Life Skills Coach Training, my work at FCSS and the work towards my personal healing continues. A lot of the therapy I am doing now focuses around my body, and how I relate to it. Once more, I lug my journal out of my bag.

May 20/88

My body is always in the way and keeps me from expressing what I feel inside. It imprisons me. It keeps me from being who I am. It does things that don't correspond to the real me. It keeps me from reaching out to people. If people reach out to me, it blocks those feelings from reaching my inner being. It acts as a barrier. To feel through my body, I detach myself from the person I really am and become a bad person, the one I felt like when I was being abused.

Who is right, my body or my inner being? Am I this bad person that my body tells me I am or is my inner being the one who's the real me? Why can't they be the same? I don't want to be two different people. I just want to be me.

Nov. 13/88

It's not okay for someone to touch me to make me feel good. Touch is only okay if it comes from someone else's needs. Then I can feel by becoming the person they need and not a person with needs.

Fortunately, my full-time work at the social agency makes it possible for me to afford to look into different healing modalities to help me move forward quicker. I work hard at healing myself, but I also work hard at being the student so one day I can be the one to help others on their personal healing journeys.

The process intrigues me and pulls me forward like a conveyor belt. It gives me a sense of purpose. My need to learn, transform, and become, is like a thirst I can't quench. I am as determined and focused as a storm chaser as I continue to seek one training after another, wanting to absorb every little bit of it. Through all of this, I continue to expand on what I offer to the community in my work at FCSS. I give workshops to groups, some for people who are grieving and another workshop I created called Friends Helping Friends, designed to teach people important skills on how to be there for others. I also continue to be faithful to my one-on-one work with Emily.

I come to her fragmented and broken looking for someone who will see beyond my tough exterior. Someone who will not be put off by my lack of words. Someone I can trust to guide me forward and someone who will love me for who I am.

Emily believes in me, the journey I am on, and what I will discover on the other side. Even when I leave my body, or get stuck in the silence, or seek help from people with alternative methods, she supports, encourages, waits for my words, and continues to help me hold the pain.

Dear One:

More questions.

I think I've lived them all, the whole gamut of emotions from A to Z. How is it possible to live such intense and varied emotions with one individual? There are many days when I ask myself how healthy or how sane that can be and I haven't really come up with an answer. But, you know what? I don't question as often anymore.

I think I've pretty much resigned myself to the fact that Emily has been, is, and will continue to be a big part of my life, and I'm okay with that. I battled this often. Me depending on someone? Me becoming vulnerable? Me speaking up?

Then there are the times where I feigned indifference to her presence in my life, but probably the only person I was kidding was myself. Now, I think, "it is what it is, and so be it."

What is that? Acceptance? Surrender? Truth? Or is it letting go of fear and opening my heart to love?

Whatever it is, it feels good. I'm quite sure I'm here to stay.

Lou

Chapter 30

Don't Touch Me

Truth creates a gentle path to healing. There is nothing to fear.

In April of 1989, before going to my Life Skills Coach training in Edmonton, I attended a workshop in Peace River.

I enter the workshop room where Neil Tubb is meeting with people individually and take a seat in the chair across from him. After some polite greetings, he studies my face for a minute and asks, "Where did your voice go? What has silenced you?"

I am floored. I try to answer the question, perhaps more so for myself than for him.

"Not everyone is patient enough to hear my words," I tell him.

"Do you want to have your voice?" he asks.

"Yes, more than anything. Yes I do!"

"It will require work on your part," he warns.

"I'm okay with that."

"What do you remember about your childhood?" is his next question.

I hesitate for a moment. "Well, some things happened with my grade one teacher when I was five years old."

He's quick to respond. "What do you remember before that, before you were five?" he asks.

I think for a minute then tell him. "Not much. Hardly anything really,"

He looks at me. "There's a book I'd like you to read. *My Father's House*, by Sylvia Fraser."

I believe everyone has experiences that only in retrospect can be seen as life changing events, that ripple their way down a cause and effect continuum that change who you are. For me, Kevin's death was one of those experiences. Seeing Emily was another, and meeting Neil that day, followed by attending his weekend healing workshop, was the third one.

That weekend marks the beginning of my quest for a series of similar healing methods. With this call to Neil and with each subsequent call I make to take part in other healing experiences, I stand in fear of the challenges I force myself to face. The question is always will I make it through—will I survive. Yet I feel compelled and drawn to these kinds of experiences.

This particular workshop, I learn from co-workers, is being led by Neil, assisted by his wife Sandra, and others from Victoria.

Neil is taking appointments and seeing people on an individual basis before his scheduled weekend workshop. I get his number and call. He agrees to see me that evening and based on the first question, "What do you remember about your childhood before the age of five, I register to take part in his weekend workshop.

At the workshop I become the observer and I learn through other people's process and experiences. I feel I am doing well but all that changes quickly when Neil decides to split us into groups and everyone is asked to participate in an exercise called "Massaging the Energy".

For this exercise, we are split into groups of three. One of us lies on a mat on the floor and the other two people massage that person's energy by moving their hands in a circular motion above the person's body and sending warm loving thoughts while remaining fully present to the person being massaged. It is a beautiful and sacred experience and for me it feels like I've entered the vision of connection and *Oneness* I had as a five-year-old child. The whole experience is imbued with love, care, and genuine presence.

After a while, we are told to switch roles and massage the energy for the second person, which is again a beautiful, sacred and life-giving experience. Then it is my turn.

Almost immediately, after my partners start working with my energy, I start to whimper, squirm, slip away. I can't stop it. I am conscious of what is going on, but in a strange kind of way, I am also detached from it and trying to understand what is happening.

Instead of being calm and relaxed, my whole body trembles like leaves in a windstorm. Neil's wife, Sandra, sees what is happening and comes running over. She motions my partners to move away and indicates she will take over. By then my body has curled into a fetal position, and the whimpers have become louder and louder. Sandra gets down on the floor beside me, scoops me up, cradles me in her arms and rocks me back and forth, back and forth like a newborn child. Tears run down my face as she continues to stroke me, holding me tight as she whispers in my ear. "Shhh, shhh, it's okay. It's okay. You're okay. You're safe. Nothing is going to happen to you. Nobody is going to touch you. I'm here. I'm here. I will stay with you. You're safe. You're okay. You're okay." I sob and sob as Sandra holds me tight, and stays with me, whispering, "Shhh, shhh, it is okay."

While I am in this vulnerable open, semi-conscious state of being, hovering between two realities, and being held in the safety of Sandra's arms, Neil comes to work with me. He urges, reassures, questions, and gently guides me to go back and relive experiences that have stolen my voice and silenced me.

I am like an animal stripped of camouflage; raw, vulnerable—easy prey. I want to run, but there is no place to run and I am too weak to move. Questions fly at me one after another. "How do you feel now? Where do you feel it? What is it you're feeling?"

It feels like vines are latching on to my throat threatening to choke out any words that might spill out of me for others to hear.

For the next half hour, while he works with me, everything is being recorded on tape. Sandra holds me, and Neil questions me, urging me to stay with it and keep moving through this painful experience. I have broken open. I have no choice but to reach deep down inside and try to come out the other side.

I am reminded of something Iyanla Vanzant said in her book *Yesterday I Cried*, which speaks to the importance of what I lived in that experience. Her words remind me that I can choose to reject or accept what happened to me. I know that accepting is always the first step to healing and to deny, as I had done in the past, would never cauterize the wounds. I could continue to bleed or I could do the healing work. I chose to do the healing work.

People can apply band aids with common addictions, even acceptable addictions like overwork, invisible addictions like sex, hidden addictions like drugs but as Vanzant says, "It will all ooze through and stain your life." I had to reach inside my own wounds, face the deepest part of the pain that held me from knowing my true self, and kept me from the *Oneness* I wanted and believed possible.

Many things were confusing, puzzling, or filled with fear and unanswered questions over the years. There was the underlying resentment I felt towards my parents when they had a drink. There was also my complete refusal to drink alcohol or to even as much as taste a drop of liquor.

Along with that, was the terrifying, paralyzing fear that choked out my words when I was around an intoxicated person. And the countless times as a child when I ran to my room, hid under the covers, pulled the pillow over my head and stuck my fingers in my ears so I would not hear Dad mumble and stumble around downstairs in a drunken stupor. All of those things, as well as the anger that exploded within me when I heard of a child being abused started to make more sense to me.

The weekend workshop with Neil helped me understand things I had lived, and I went to my journal to try to decipher it all.

April 29/89

Dad, when I visited at your place some time ago, you and I sat in the living room watching TV together. A program about people who experienced sexual abuse came on. I felt a need then to tell you about my grade one teacher and how he touched me in inappropriate ways, but when I looked at you something told me that it was best not to, that you would not be able to hear what I had to say.

For a moment I resented this, but as I looked at you and saw you reach for another drink, saw the tears in your eyes, and saw you put a nitro pill under your tongue to ease your heart pains, I knew I would not be able to share my pain with you.

I couldn't understand then the depth of the pain you were feeling, but I understand now that you were sitting in your own pain, your pain of things past and I understand now that my pain started even before I went to school because someone else other than my schoolteacher messed with my body. I don't have a clear image of who that person was and perhaps it's not as important that I know who with 100% certainty; what matters more, is that I acknowledge what happened and that I heal from it as best I can.

I understand more about the confusion and the emptiness I felt inside now. It was hard to remember, to go back to a piece of me tucked away in far corners of my mind, memories of another world, another me, a me I couldn't go to before because the pain was too great to go there alone.

Yesterday, the vision I have had ever since the age of five, became real for me. While taking part in an experiential workshop, I was surrounded by some powerful energy that kept me safe enough to reach into those memories. I was held by a force, a love that surrounded and supported me, and acted as a light that allowed me to travel back through time and face the pain I feared would swallow me, and plunge me forever into the depths of darkness.

Maybe you can't understand the pain you feel sometimes, and maybe you've never had the strength or support to look at why it's there or how to heal from it. I don't know, and it's not that important that I know, but it is crucial that I learn how to be free.

There is a place I go, a place that is safe, warm, soft and receiving. I'd like to bring you with me. It's a place where we could let ourselves love each other the way it should have been in the past.

The way I'd like it to be now. The way it should have always been. I am choosing to move through memories and to move towards making peace. I wish I could do the same for you.

Dear One:

This is crazy. One minute I say this whole abuse stuff can't be true. The next minute I know it being true explains a lot of things. All those things didn't come out of nowhere.

Yes, it is true. No, it isn't. Yes, it is. I'm like a tennis ball bounced from one end of the court to the other!

A mass of feelings engulfs me, swirls and sneaks around like steam escaping above the shower door. Where do I belong amongst this jungle of thoughts, feelings, and emotions? And how does all this bring me any closer to the Oneness I'm reaching for?

Fuck the damn abuse and what it's done to me! Fuck it all anyway!

Lou

Chapter 31

Diving Deeper

If there is a secret to mental health, it is to open the door on secrets.

In November of 1989, I flew to Victoria, BC, to work with Neil in private sessions.

I stay at his home on the island. After our one-on-one sessions, I spend time in nature, reflecting, and processing what I am living.

I work hard. Some work focuses on the abuse and some work revolves around Kevin's death. Each day brings a new level of awareness, and an acceptance of realities.

When it gets difficult, I can feel my body tense, and then it is as if I am outside of myself, and looking down watching what I am going through. I don't want to separate. I want to be one. One whole person. One with me, one with the present moment, and one with my outside world.

With Neil's help and with my pen, I move forward through the quicksand of an understanding of things that have stood in my way.

Nov 8/89

Talking about what happened to me makes me feel like I'm the one who is betraying rather than the one who was betrayed. Secrecy does that. It binds you in guilt and shame and silences you. My journey now is to allow the hurt to surface, to release the anger and to free myself from the clutches of guilt and shame. It's a gradual climb up a steep hill.

The feeling that there are two of me, invades me. There's one that is good and one that is bad, and I fear one will contaminate the other. It's all so damn hard and complicated because we are stuck inside the same body—a stupid body that only adds to my confusion because sometimes it needs loving and touching and sometimes the loving and touching feels good and sometimes it hurts and I don't know which me it belongs to.

All I want is to figure this out, to peel away the shame that has wrapped itself around my soul like a fog that obliterates the sun. All I want is to connect with the real me, the one who started out to just "be" in this world.

There's nothing wrong with my body. It's what was done to it that was wrong. I didn't have the power to control that, but oh how I've tried to have power and control over everything since.

I tried to keep part of me submerged below the surface. I fought against myself to never shed a tear or to never let what I felt inside make itself known on the outside, but the power is mine now and it's time I let the real me out!

When I leave Neil's place, I know there is still work to do. Healing, like building a house, happens one step at a time. At least now, I'm beginning to learn the importance of nurturing and loving the child that once was just that—a child.

Diving deep below the surface to touch on and release the pain that accumulated over the years swings the door open a little further, allowing more light to come in, and by the time the end of November rolls around, I feel like I'm an inch taller. I walk with more determination and there's a bounce to my step that wasn't there before. I've let go of some of the load I've lugged around in my pack sack for so long.

Nov 28/89

I used to think I was a big dreamer, but I don't anymore. There are others who see life as an experience to be lived, to learn from and to be open to. I've seen others want and seek the same as me and I've even shared the experience with others so I know I'm not alone. I'm not crazy for sticking with those dreams.

The feeling that I am meant to do something that I haven't even touched yet, that there is more than what I am living now is always with me. I never quite know what that something is, but this yearning for more has been with me ever since I can remember.

I keep thinking that there must be a reason for everything I've lived through, and continue to live through, and that there's a power greater than myself that guides and urges me to move forward. More and more I feel a Presence of, of... of what? I don't even know.

I've never been a religious person and this Presence doesn't have a religious context or name for me—except maybe to call it Oneness.

When I am out in nature, the many shapes and colors of the trees, the trickle of the water in the creek, the formation of clouds, how the stars sparkle and shine in the sky, the rich colors of a rainbow after a rain, the sunrise and sunset, the birds, the animals—all of that brings me close to, and in communion with, this Presence and I can feel this Oneness and the search I'm on now is to deepen this sense of Oneness and truth within me.

I want to reach even deeper into it. There's something going on inside me that I can only describe as a yearning to guide people who, like me, feel a need to connect to their truth and maybe even live this sense of Oneness that I speak of.

The yearning is so strong, yet every now and then, I hear The Shaming voice in the background saying, "Have you gone mad? Just who do you think you are?"

I think I may slap that, "Have you gone mad? Just who do you think you are?" voice upside the head and tell it to shut up!

Before I know it, it's January and time to leave for the training. I am determined to learn, grow, and acquire skills I can bring back to my work at FCSS. I'm on a mission to bring meaning and purpose to my life, and I believe that one way I can do this is by guiding others on their personal journey.

The training is intense, demanding, at times grueling and all consuming, but I am determined to see it through. I need to do this as much as I need to breathe.

A week in and I am challenged. Danny asks me to voice what I feel about something that has just happened in group. I look at my classmates sitting around the circle and try to speak up, but when I try to form the words, no words come, and I hear Danny say, "I don't think you'd say shit if your mouth was full of it."

My face turns red. There's no way to ignore this. Which feelings to hold back? Which to let through? Feelings. They can't be segregated like cattle in a chute where only chosen ones are let through. This is the moment. All or nothing. They wait, I struggle pushing past the shame and locked doors.

With every word I speak The Shaming Voice pipes in. "What the hell are you doing breaking the silence?" At first the confusion and pain that come with disclosing is almost as painful as the secret itself.

While my outer voice is being heard, The Shaming voice continues to scream at me, "What are you thinking? How are you ever going to take back what you are saying? How are you going to put the cat back in the bag? You're going to destroy your family." On and on The Shaming Voices go until I hear my other voice, the one that is actually speaking and sharing my truth out loud end with,

"And that's what happened to me."

Silence.

The voices are gone.

There's just me.

Alone.

Standing.

The group leaders suggest I take part in a sexual abuse group while I am in Edmonton, I have already registered. I am attending my second evening of a six-week group meeting that night and there too, group therapy is intense. The group often demands every ounce of energy I have left after my day of training with Life Skills. By the time I leave the sexual abuse group, I am toast.

On one particular night, the meeting ends and I walk out to my car like a zombie. It's the night we have been asked to write a letter to our abuser. I turn the key. Pull out into the street and I go blank. I have no idea where I am. No idea where I'm going. I drive around a few blocks. Nothing looks familiar. I try to read the little green numbered signs. They blur. They don't make sense. I panic.

I shouldn't be alone. I don't know who I can be with. I know no one. I have no phone. I have no one to call. I try to think about where I am staying. A friend of the family. An elderly lady. She's sleeping. I don't remember her address. I just know how to get there. Or used to. North side of city. Yes, that's it! North side. Somewhere. I want to stop the car to think but I'm on a bridge. I can't stop. It dumps me on the South side. I need to turn around. Think. Think. I need to get home. Tears sting my eyes making it even harder to see. I have to pull over. Calm down. Take deep breaths. I have to do this. There's no one to help me.

It takes me over an hour. I open the door, tip-toe in and drop on the couch fully clothed. My head spins as I whisper a few words of gratitude. Then I pass out.

The following week when I go to the sexual abuse group, the evening is lighter. This time we are asked to write a letter to our inner child.

Dear Ti-Lou:

Shame and guilt taught me to see you with contempt and loathing - to see you as a tainted helpless child. I have shut you out of my existence, ignored you, and alienated myself from you. You became virtually non-existent to others and often even to myself.

I concealed you under layers of pretense, masks I wore and roles I played. I tried to ignore your screams and your battle and it became less and less okay to even as much as acknowledge you.

I was expected to be an adult functioning in an adult world. Even when you tugged at my pant leg, I could not understand. How could a child with wants, needs and fears be a part of me when I was supposed to be an adult?

Maybe you're the one who stopped me from running around in circles and urged me to start peeling back the layers. It was hard to acknowledge you when you were surrounded with so much fear but I hear you now and you're likely the reason I never gave up.

I understand your fear. It's okay. Whatever you feel - it's okay. You can let go. I will not abandon you. You are who I am meant to be because deep inside, you hold the essence of who I am.

Lou

By taking part in the sexual abuse group, I make several important discoveries about my need to be connected to people at a heart level.

Jan. 15/90

For me needing someone is extremely dangerous. It robs me of my power and it puts me at risk of being dependent. Right now, that's what I live with Emily and I suspect that is also the case with Garry sometimes. So part of my anger is at myself because I need someone, and the other part of my anger is at those I care for because needing someone feels like I'm being robbed of my power and that just throws me back into feeling abused all over again.

I strive to make it on my own which, in many ways, is a good thing, but it is not a good thing when it keeps those I love from getting close to me. I need to learn that being able to receive is a gift to others as much as giving to others is a gift to me.

By the end of March 1990, I graduate. I have survived the two-month intensive training and am now officially a Life Skills Coach and darn proud of it. As demanding and grueling as the training was, it was also very life giving and I am going home with more confidence, tools, insight, skills and knowledge to help me in my work with people. I jump into creating workshops and offering them in the community.

I have learned a lot, both professionally and personally, and in many ways, I have shifted and grown. I have let go of trying to change Garry and I feel I am more tender, more understanding with my children. My energy has even shifted with my mother-in-law. I feel stronger and I don't take things as personally as I once did.

Although I still have to dig to the bottom of my boots to find the courage to use my voice, at least I am taking risks to say how I feel and to speak from my heart. I can stand in my truth, and I can speak my words out loud but I doubt I will ever transform into an extrovert.

Standing in my truth, however, means I also have more to face.

Dear One:

To release all fears, to stand alone in the nakedness of my truth; to be truth itself; I've been trying to figure out what that would hold for me?

Freedom, spaciousness, spontaneity, and connection on deeper levels. Those are the rewards I imagine I could reap if I stood in the truth of who I am. It all sounds pretty good to me. So what stops me then? Is it the thought of never being able to bring others to understand what it is I live, the thought of rejection, or maybe even the loss of those I love and hold dear?

I know; I'm full of questions again. But I need to ask.

Right now, even if it leads to the unknown, it's harder and more painful to stay where I am than to move to truths.

When I was out for a walk this morning I asked myself: what does standing in my truth mean for me? What does it awaken?

The answer was my sexuality, and what that awakens is scary.

I keep hearing those words that Emily often said to me, "The truth will set you free," and right now I'm thinking if I'm to take a step forward with the truth that lies within me, I sure hope you will be "the One" to stand by me.

Lou

Chapter 32

Always Questioning

There's no need for me to be other than who I am.

I looked up the address. I found the place on the city map, got in my car and headed out. Enough imagining, enough wondering. It was time to do something, anything.

I drive downtown to 106th Street and 105th Avenue, slow down then spot the building. I don't know what I expected, but it doesn't look any different from the other buildings. I check the address again. Yes, it is the right building but instead of parking, I drive around the block, once, twice, three times, while I keep jabbering aloud.

"What are you so scared of. Park the darn car and make yourself go in. No one is going to eat you, for God's sake. Don't be such a coward. Pull up your socks. Just go already!"

I lean my head back on the headrest and take several deep breaths to center and ground myself as I have been taught to do in my trainings. I reach for the door handle with my right hand and grab my wallet with my left hand. Then I freeze. My wedding rings! I can't go in there with my wedding ring. People will notice and wonder what I'm doing there?

I slip the rings off my finger, put them in my wallet where I keep my change, take a couple of deep breaths, force myself to leave the security of my car and make my way across the street.

"Am I supposed to knock? Do I just walk in? Will someone greet me? What will I say? What if there's something going on, like a private function, or I need a membership or something? Then what? Do I just say sorry and turn around and leave?"

My heart attempts to jump out of my chest as I make my way up the steps, turn the doorknob and slowly push the door open.

A middle-aged man with dark brown hair and blue eyes greets me. "Hi, is this your first time here?" he asks.

"It is." I respond.

"Well welcome, it's a pleasure to meet you," he says as he extends his hand to take mine. "Come, I'll show you around. This is one of our mixed nights when both men and women attend our LGBT center. Wednesday nights are women only. There's a list of upcoming events and everything that's happening at the center in this pamphlet. Here's our lending library full of books and videos. Over here is our activity room, and this is our little cafeteria nook. Grab a coffee, a tea, browse around, mingle. If you have questions, we're here."

People are welcoming, but I have to dig deep to make conversation and as soon as I can, I excuse myself and make my way to the library room. Two memoirs, written by women coming to term with their sexuality, jump off the shelf. I sign the books out, say goodbye and make a quick exit with the books tucked under my arm.

Dear One:

If I was made into a sexual being, then I am deserving of being loved in a sexual way, aren't I?

If I was made into a sexual being, then having sexual feelings, no matter what they are, doesn't make me a bad person, does it?

If I was made into a sexual being, it is okay for my body to need, and to have those needs met by someone, isn't it?

Being a sexual being, I should be loved for who I am and not for what my body can do for someone else, right?

Being a sexual being is part of who I am, just like being emotional or spiritual is part of who I am, isn't it?

Being a sexual being means yet another way to be one with someone else, right?

Always questioning.

Lou

Chapter 33

Surrender

My truth can be different than your truth, but what will be the same is the place it comes from, and how it feels when we get there.

Just as it's hard to know joy if you've never known sadness, it is hard to live truth unless it encompasses everything. And the truth about my sexuality was bubbling to the surface.

There are days where I think I will go crazy. I don't understand the feelings I have. They are so powerful, it frightens me. Not so much the feelings themselves but what it means if I pay attention to those feelings.

Part of me aches to be free to let go and to love freely and another part of me says, "You can't do that!" My body is caught in a tug of war. I don't know where I belong. I scream into the emptiness that surrounds me, "I want to be me, whatever the hell that is. I just want to be me!"

There are times when I hate myself for the way I feel, and I try to distance from my feelings, but I can't pick and choose to feel one thing and not another. If I allow myself to feel, then I have to feel it all, and that includes the reality that keeps staring me in the face asking to be acknowledged.

Sometimes I look at women and wonder what it would be like to be with them, and just as quickly I push the thoughts as far back as I can. I am not supposed to have those kinds of thoughts, especially not when I am a married woman that birthed four children. But the thoughts and feelings keep popping up like weeds.

Why, do I always end up in a place where it's so hard to be true to myself?

Endless questions I try to answer.

March 13/94

All my life I've carried secrets around. Enough! I need to be free from this ball and chain.

Freedom. Is there such a thing? Are we ever free? I wish I was. I wish I could soar like an eagle.

I still fight with the demons of abuse that tell me that feeling good in my body means feeling bad about myself.

Right now, I am as fragile as a bubble. If anyone touches me, I will splatter into nothingness. This person inside me frightens me, yet warms me. She confuses me, yet brings me peace. She makes me vulnerable, yet solidifies me. There's a need to protect her, and also keep her hidden, and at the same time there's a need to let her exist and come alive.

I hurt so bad it feels like my heart is being ripped out of my chest one sinew at a time, yet I have to smile and pretend.

Holding back throughout my life. Why do I constantly find myself having to hold back?

Growing up I watched my mom hold back and I thought that's what I had to do too. Sometimes the abuse felt good in my body but I held back because I knew it was wrong. Going out on dates, I held back sexually because I wasn't supposed to be sexual. Now I hold back from showing love because what I feel is so intense and my intensity scares people. I hold back my anger, my hurt, and on and on it goes. I'm always holding back.

My whole body aches with the need to express and feel. It cries in agony not knowing how to be set free. It is hungry with desire, has a mind of its own, and often tries to rule. Waves of need rush in. A steady rhythm that undermines the shore of my resistance.

How can I trust my body, its needs and what it is telling me? How can I trust the signs, the unrelenting desire that is like a relentless toothache that won't go away? What I feel are the cries of a hungry body and of loneliness. When I travel away from home, I find myself stealing glances at women in a desiring way. What I want is to love and be loved and to have a woman's body next to mine.

My heart goes out to a Vietnam War veteran, Leonard P. Matlovich. His words ignite every cell in my body. "For killing two men I got a medal of honor. For loving one man – I got a dishonorable discharge."

My insides ache. I cry. I pull out my journal.

April 26/95

I sit at home tonight. My body in a ravaged mood. A deep inner longing consumes me. And if I am honest with my words and myself, what I want and desire more than anything else, is to be in the company of a woman.

This is what I desire, crave and need. I am not willing to deny it any longer but I haven't a clue what to do with the insatiable hunger and unquenchable thirst that constantly ravages my body and the depths of my being.

It's no wonder I have difficulty finding my voice and expressing my passionate self when I restrain and deny my own reality in an effort to be what I think others expect.

This is me, take it or leave it, love me or hate me, agree with me or not. This is who I am. Today, I stand before these pages naked in my truth. Now I need to learn how to stand in my truth before the rest of the world.

Over and over I have been told by those who are part of my healing journey not to deny, ignore. "What you resist persists," I often keep hearing. I believe that, too, but when it comes to my body, I fail to see how to apply this knowledge, or if it even applies at all. When I allow myself to feel, it magnifies the needs of my body even more.

Does what I feel about my sexuality work like grief, or anger, or any other emotion? If I dive in and stay with it, if I allow myself to go to the center, stay present to all the feelings until I am the feelings themselves, will they let go of me then? Will the feelings slowly disappear?

My fear is that diving in will not free me. I am trapped within a needy body and there are times I wish I could discard it like an unwanted piece of scrap metal and go pick out a new one. I hear Emily say, "Don't try to control, let go, allow,"

"And just how am I supposed to do that?"

How can I live closeness, the need for touch, companionship, connection, love, and *Oneness* with another when I can't live it within my relationship?

The more I look at it the more acute the need becomes. Even writing about it makes the need take on a life of its own. At least I no longer judge, condemn, blame, or make my body wrong or bad. I accept. Maybe that is enough of a step forward for now.

Dear One:

I had to come to Edmonton this weekend to attend a training and tonight I went to see a therapist who deals specifically with sexual identity issues. It feels good to be able to talk about and be acknowledged in what I feel and live. It has brought everything even closer to the surface and it doesn't work very well to try to push it away anymore.

All my life the message I've received is to either hold back or deny what I see or feel. I am unwilling to continue to put that same pressure on myself. There is nothing wrong with what I feel. Nothing. Absolutely nothing!

There are millions of people who feel the way I do. For all I know there could even be someone living the same thing who lives right next door, who suppresses, denies or fears claiming who they are.

Why shouldn't we feel what we feel, talk about, share, explore and enjoy the totality of who we are including our sexuality?

When we pretend on the outside to be someone other than who we are inside, nothing that comes to us feels real because we are not being real ourselves. Pretense only leads to loneliness and resentments. Well, I'm done.

"Follow your heart. Live as who you are. Be true to yourself." It's what I teach; it's what I believe; it's what I want for myself and it's what I know is important. All my life I've felt a need to discover truth and to live authentically. This is the threshold I'm standing on now. What do I do with this truth I've awakened to—the one that says I love women and the knowledge that this is where I belong now and maybe always have?

Perhaps the confusion I've been living is not so much about my sexuality but more about the refusal to see things for what they really are?

The word "surrender" flashes on and off like an "open" sign in a restaurant. Surrender is the answer. Feeling One with, I hope will be the result.

Lou

Chapter 34

Travel, Training & Transitions

Habit keeps me in the same place, change moves me forward.

After my Life Skill Coach training, I felt much more confident and better-equipped to do effective work with clients in my position at FCSS.

With my training paid for, I am committed to give back to the community by offering the workshops I promised to deliver. I spend countless hours building and preparing as though my life depends on it, then I jump in before I can lose my nerve. But, no matter how prepared I am, when the time comes to present I have to muster all the courage I have to pull it off. Thank God for Emily and my co-workers who support and believe in me and what I can do.

The fear is great, but the need to give in ways that matter, the need to make a difference and to live my truth is even greater. And each time I put myself out there, stretch beyond my comfort zone, and manage to find a way to go through the fear, little by little, it gets better. Thoughts of what I was like in the very first workshop

I participated in reassure me that, even if it's still challenging, I have come a long way.

The workshops I give are well received and the work I do one-on-one with clients is also going well and the amount of people I see is steadily increasing. There are moments where I have doubts and fears but I absolutely love what I do. I feel more alive than I ever have. I want more.

It worked the first time so I figure it's worth another shot. I try again. I approach the board for more training with the promise that I will deliver more programs and workshops and the assurance that further training will also help me deepen my work with clients. They agree. I am ecstatic.

During the ten years I work for FCSS, I am fortunate enough to take part in numerous short trainings, which include trainings with Helen Bass, one of the authors of A Courage to Heal, a workshop with Wayne Dyer, suicide prevention training, grief and loss, self-esteem, an inner child workshop, journal writing, and many more trainings that are helpful in my work.

Although the trainings are all good, two of those trainings make a huge difference in my life, and give me a lot to give back to the community. For both of these trainings, my colleague and I travel to Seattle and to The Omega Institute in New York. One training is called the *Art of Empowerment*. It's a professional training in facilitating human potential given by David Gershon and Gail Straub. The other training given by someone else is called *Healing the Child Within*. Both my co-worker and I come back pumped and ready to offer empowerment workshops in the Municipal District.

I continue to train but I also continue with Emily. Everything I can learn, inform myself with or heal with, I seek out and try. I am like a storm chaser in a desert. I have a thirst I can't quench to learn more about people, the human psyche, how to grow and create change and I seek one experience after another. I also take part in writing courses. I am fascinated by the power of the written word and what it can do for people, and the powerful role it's already played in my own journey.

Three different times I meet with a highly intuitive and gifted lady who does Cranio-sacral therapy, and another time I meet with a lady who does hypnosis. Emily accompanies me to these sessions. Having her witness my process with these experiences allows her to understand me better and helps her in the work she continues to do with me.

These highly intuitive and gifted women I work with are people who have never seen me before. They don't know anything about me except for my name when I walk through their door. After working with me, they both confirm the abuse, and what I have lived through as a result.

Then in August of 1992, when I am in the middle of working hard at preparing and putting together a ten-week group for survivors of sexual abuse, I hear of yet another innocent little girl we know who has been touched in inappropriate ways and I go into a tailspin. It is yet another confirmation that the abuse I experienced isn't a fabrication of my imagination. I can no longer hang on to the last little thread of doubt I desperately want to hang on to that maybe it wasn't true. I can no longer deny the truth.

I am filled with anger, resentment and hurt, so much hurt for the little girl this happened to and for the little girl I once was. Another innocent little girl suffers, and a man with too much to drink, is to blame. For the first time in my life, I share with my sisters that this also happened to me.

Two years later, 1994 rolls around and it is a year packed with changes both with my work and at home. Some are a little scary but I thrive on change and it feels exhilarating. FCSS is undergoing some major transitions and my work of the past ten years is coming to a close.

On the home front, our three daughters are growing and going through some changes as well. Our oldest daughter Karen, has graduated from grade twelve with honors, awards and scholarships. Throughout high school Karen has been a high achiever, mover, shaker, hard worker and go-getter. She has rallied for the underdog, led peer support groups, and, even against the voices of many, organized a dry grad for those who wanted to attend. Now this young woman is about to graduate from the University of Alberta with a Master's Degree in Education and is making plans for her approaching wedding day.

Our second daughter Jody, the social one with a more relaxed, easy-going kind of attitude about life, and a high achiever, is leaving in September to attend Grant MacEwan College in Edmonton to study to be a Travel Consultant—studies that will later land her a job with West Jet Airlines.

Brenda, the youngest one, is quiet, reserved, good humored and disciplined, and she will be the only one remaining at home. She has made the decision not to attend high school but to pursue her studies for grades ten to twelve on her own through distance education.

Both Garry and I can't be any prouder of our girls, not only for what they have accomplished, but also for the beautiful young women all three of them have grown into and become. There are a lot of changes happening on the outside but a lot of changes are taking place inside, too.

The relationship Garry and I share is held together by routine, a sense of conformity and a certain level of resignation to living our life in a way that has become the norm. When it comes to living a sense of connection and closeness, I feel as empty and as barren as prairie land can sometimes be. We live in two different worlds. Our conversations center on our children or the land we farm. Apart from that, we no longer speak the same language. And the less I feel connected at home, the more I search to connect elsewhere.

.

Dear One:

Do you know how grateful I am for the learning, the new experiences, and yes, even the challenges that have come my way? I may not be any taller on the outside but I have grown so much on the inside.

I am not only grateful, but humbled as well, to have had and to continue to have the opportunity to sit in a sacred space with people, listen to their stories and work with them to recognize the beauty of who they are and to reach their full potential. It's a privilege I feel extremely honored to have.

For all of that, I am grateful.

Lou

Chapter 35

Defining Moments

I am woman – I am man – I am spirit – I am soul – I am not – who I've been told.

For twenty years, I was faithful in my marriage, then one night all that changed. About a month before FCSS closed its doors and I opened my bookstore, I met someone.

From the moment I see her I am mesmerized. She is a goddess, a petite woman with an Australian accent, blond hair down to her waist and brown eyes that sparkle like morning dew. I am busy talking with a client when, out of the corner of my eye, I catch sight of her asking the receptionist if she can browse through our self-help library.

My undivided attention with my client I've been engaged in conversation with is compromised. Where I want to be is at the front desk where I could find out more about the woman who is browsing through the books and has succeeded in pulling me in, without even glancing my way. Her voice, her accent, her laughter is like music to my ears and I am curious to learn more about her.

What books is she taking out? Where does she come from? Where does she live, and when will she be back I wonder.

I hear her laugh at something the secretary says, and then I see her steal a glance in my direction. Her smile makes my heart turn cartwheels and I silently curse the fact that I am busy now and for the rest of the day.

I am intrigued; not only by this woman, but also by the reaction I am having to her. I have to find out more about her. The client I am with is about to leave, but my next client is walking in and there is no time to introduce myself. My only hope is the contact information she is required to leave in order to take books home with her.

When I emerge from my counselling office an hour later, I hurry over to the front desk and ask, "Who was that woman who checked all those books out earlier? Where is she from? What did she have to say?" The receptionist smiles at me and pulls out her library card and there it is, a contact phone number which gives me a general idea of the area where she lives and her name. It's Madison.

I quickly jot down the phone number on a piece of paper and tuck it in my pocket. "The next time she comes into the office," I tell the girl at the desk, "promise you'll let me know right away."

I have no idea what is happening to me. I have never reacted to anyone this way before, and I don't know why I am reacting like this now. All I know is that I have to meet this woman. I have to talk with her, and hopefully, maybe even get to know her. For the next two weeks, I obsess about calling her even if I have no idea what I can possibly say that would explain why I am calling.

Two weeks later the secretary pokes her head around the corner into my office and announces, "She's here!" My heart takes a nose dive into the pit of my stomach. I feel like a crazy teenager about to go on a date with the head of the cheer leading team.

"Make sure you hold her attention and don't let her leave until I get there," I tell her as I dash off to the washroom to take a quick look in the mirror in case I have lettuce stuck in my teeth or hairs sticking out of my ears. Then, with all the confidence I can gather, I square my shoulders, walk to the front office and introduce myself to this woman. Unknown to both of us, we are about to start a relationship.

The pull in the beginning is her long hair, her sensuous smile, her Australian accent, her long slender legs, the necklaces she wears that allow my eyes to drift to the outline of her breasts, and her laughter like that of a carefree child. The pull is her total rapture in poets like Leonard Cohen, artists like Matisse and musicians like Dutch Tilders and Louis Armstrong. The pull is her total innocence in simple matters like changing a tire or balancing a check book and her complete competence in other matters like living in hostels, how to ski down a mountain or heal a sick llama. The pull is her intense way of feeling her way through life. The pull is how elegant she can look even in her most rugged and casual wear while working on the farm or when she's all dressed up to go out on the town. The pull is how attractive she looks with her Jacaru hat, leather backpack over her right shoulder, her UGG boots, her three-quarter length coat, her dangling earrings and a smile that makes me melt inside.

I ask if it is okay with her if I call, and over the next few months, we get to know each other. We meet at a coffee shop, we go out for lunch, I visit at her place and sometimes help her do things around the yard while we talk. We discover we both studied the same kind of courses, we love the same kind of books, the same kind of music, we both share a love for the written word, the outdoors, animals and nature. We are drawn to each other like opposing ends of a magnet, but we are also both married.

Whenever we can, we meet face to face and if that isn't possible, we spend hours and hours getting to know each other by talking on the phone. Then, as I usually do every year, I plan a trip to visit my family, and I extend an invitation for her to join me. She agrees. We make plans.

I work until four and we make arrangements to meet in Whitecourt. We arrive almost at the same time. I transfer her bags from the bus to my car and we head out. Since our schedule doesn't allow for an early start for the twelve-to fourteen-hour trip to Kelowna, the plan is to split the trip in two by staying overnight somewhere. We will be together. Alone.

We stop a few times for bathroom breaks and gas and when she gets in or out of the car, I open the door for her. While driving, we share stories, discuss life and the living of it, listen to music, and drive through the mountains holding hands.

I can feel her hair as she leans over to pull some CDs from her leather bag to slide into the player. The sound of Muddy Waters fills the spaces between our laughter, our words and our hearts. All my senses are heightened and I feel alive. The sun is shining on the snow-capped mountains, the creeks are roaring and flowing to capacity and we admire the elk and mountain goats on the side of the road as we drive by. It is a beautiful evening with a steady breeze that tries to whisper words of caution in my ear, but they are drowned by the excitement that builds within me and the need for total abandonment.

Just as the sun tucks away behind the mountain range and the night sky pulls the shades over the brightness of the day, I pull into a small town, find a motel with a vacancy sign and book us in for the night.

I walk back to the car with key in hand feeling light-headed. It feels like I am playing a part in a movie. Everything is surreal as if my feet are gliding on water. I can't figure out if it is due to having eaten very little supper, or if it is some kind of sixth sense trying to warn me that when I turn the key in that lock, and walk over that threshold, it will forever alter my life as I have known it so far, but whatever it is, I choose to ignore it.

I slide in beside her under the covers and our stories continue as she rests in the crook of my arm.

"Sorry," she says.

"Sorry for what?" I ask.

"I touched your breast. It was an accident, I swear," she responds.

"I wish it hadn't been," I say, as I reach for her hand and place it on my breast again. "It's okay," I say. "It's okay."

She turns her head, looks at me and when our eyes meet, we both realize we are about to descend to a place from which there can be no return. I take her. She takes me. Everyone and everything else falls away and there is only us. Alone, but together. Two of us connected as *One*.

From the time I met her in the fall of 95 and the first time we spent the night together, it completely changes me, or perhaps more accurately, brings into alignment the truth of who I am. Even in my journal I can't find the words to describe the depth of what I am living, but I know, from that moment on, that my world as I have known it so far, has been changed forever.

I am forty-three years old, and for the first time in my life, I find myself in a place of deep meaningful connection. I have connected to, and fallen in love with this woman at a body, spirit, and soul level and as a result life takes on a deeper, fuller meaning than I have ever experienced before.

In my journal, I write these words:

Sometimes I think how I feel must be written all over my face. I keep thinking, how could anyone not see it when inside I'm glowing like a humongous Christmas tree.

She captivates me and I fall to a place of no return. For the first time in my life, I so desperately need and want to climb the rooftops and shout my joy to the world, and I can't. Instead, she, and the way I feel about her, become my secret life, the part I can't talk about. The circumstances of our situation, bind us to secrecy, and it's the secrecy part that doesn't sit well with me. It's a pattern that has all too often been a part of my life. I have tried so hard to free myself. Once more I find myself smack in the middle of secrecy.

I see her smile, hear her voice, and time stands still for me. She totally consumes me. Her voice, her touch, her smell, her looks follow me everywhere, every waking minute of the day and rob me of sleep at night. I am convinced that something as beautiful and as powerful as what I live with her is meant to be. I am prepared to be true to who I am and to somehow find a way to make it work. But, that is how I feel.

"I tried to love her my way but I couldn't make it hold," a line from one of Leonard Cohen's songs, a reminder, among many, of how my time with her is. She is like water slipping through my fingers. She can't believe in me.

I give all I have, but it is never enough. It can never be enough to erase her past hurts or to fill the gaping big hole of abandonment that has followed her through the years. She sees me not as I am, but as who she believes me to be, another Hannah, another Liam, another Rebecca, who will eventually hurt and abandon her even though I am prepared to risk everything for her. Despite all the warning signs I cannot change her perception. I move forward into the midst of the flames and try to carry her like a princess in the palm of my hand.

We go places together, we hike, see movies, attend workshops, write, share stories about our life, our families, what we like and don't like, in-laws, farming, poetry, music, and art.

We discuss, debate, and philosophize about the mystery and the beauty of life, of human beings and of the human spirit. We laugh, cry, we love, we comfort one another and all of it is beautiful and means the world to me. And then, boom! It explodes, and what moments before were rapturous and life-giving moments turn into misunderstandings that I can't talk or fight my way out of. Madison can fling words off the tip of her tongue while I struggle to dredge them out from beneath a landslide.

"How could you take off and leave me?"

"But, that was the plan?"

"You just dumped me and took off. You didn't even stay. You took off!"

"What? I ....."

"You didn't wait. You didn't ask if I wanted to stay? You didn't give a hoot about me. You didn't ask if I wanted to come."

"But..., we had already...."

"Already what? Already decided in your head?"

"No, we already discussed I would stay at my daughter's. I thought...."

"No, you didn't think. You don't care. It didn't make any difference to you I had nowhere to go, no way to leave. I was stuck."

"But...but, Hannah's your friend. You were eager to see her. You said you had lots to catch up on, and...."

"Ya well, some friend you are? You say you love me, yet you leave me and don't come back until morning?"

"But, we decided before. Me at Karen's, you with Hannah. I would have...."

"You would have what? Have it convenient for you?"

"No. Have loved to have you stay with me."

"Right! You didn't stay, you left. I didn't even have Karen's number. What kind of friend does that—say you care, dump me and leave!"

"Dump you?"

"Ya, dump me! Did you spend the night?"

"No."

"Well then?"

"Madison, I came in, met Hannah, visited and stuck with the plan."

"Plan, plan! If you cared at all you would have changed your plan."

"My plan? It was our...."

"You're so selfish. You only think about you. You don't care how I feel or what I want. Who does that to someone they care about?"

"Selfish? I wanted you with me but you wanted to spend time with Hannah."

"Yes, you're selfish. I didn't even have a way to reach you. You just don't care!"

"Madison, what happened?"

"We had to share the bed, She made advances. I had to huddle in the corner by the wall all night. I didn't move. Didn't sleep. You show up with a smile. This is your fault. Take me home."

The silence of our four hour trip is broken only by other traffic rushing by and the gusts of wind that sway the car back and forth. My spirit is crushed.

When things are going well between us, I feel like I hold the world in my hands. Then things spin out of control. I can't hang on. One minute I know exactly what I have to do, the next minute I grope and stumble around in the dark trying to find where I belong. Guessing games, riddles, words with double meanings make my head spin. I need things to be straightforward, simple and clear.

These misunderstandings ambush me and without knowing what they are really about, none of my truth makes a difference. She feels unloved and is adamant that I don't care when nothing can be further from the truth. But when I try to speak, she either doesn't want to hear me, or my difficulty expressing myself makes me dig myself further and further down the rabbit-hole.

Our relationship can go from hot to cold in a few minutes, and every time it happens I shrink back a little further and I am a little more gun-shy. Regardless, I keep hoping and trying.

Dear One:

I take a step forward and it seems like I go back two.
It's not in my heart to hurt or create pain.
All I want is to love and be loved, but I am failing miserably.
Lou

Chapter 36

Finding My Footing

I am not a master of truth. I am a student, who like everyone else struggles to bring truth into my life.

While I struggled with my intense and often difficult relationship with Madison, everything else in my life continued. It was a lot to manage and juggle.

I am still very much a part of all the farming. The hours are long and often demanding but the sight of the Northern Lights dancing in the sky as I make my way back and forth across the field working the land, or the satisfaction of looking behind and seeing the land ready for the next crop gives me joy.

Our yard and garden requires continuous maintenance but it can also be a welcome distraction as well as a source of life when I get to spend my day outside under a hot summer sun. There's nothing like the smell of fresh cut grass, the snap of a pea pod popping open, or the taste of a big juicy carrot fresh out of the ground that I wipe clean on my pant leg before I bite down.

But, there's always more. The grocery shopping, washing clothes, the daily upkeep of a household, making meals, or driving the girls to baseball, swimming, skating, birthday parties. Then there's the farming bookwork to keep up with, not to mention, going to work at my job. Sometimes I can't wait for the sun to drop down and the moon to signal the close of the day.

Karen, and Jody are furthering their studies in Edmonton and I make the occasional trip to the city to spend time with them. Brenda is doing well with school, but her health is not going so well.

"Mom, I don't feel good."

"Why? What's going on?"

"My heart. It's beating fast again. It feels like it will jump out of my chest. It hurts."

I go to her and put my hand on her chest for a second but even before I do, I can see her shirt pulsing up and down. I take her pulse. I can barely count the beats.

"Concentrate on your breath. Try to slow your heart down. Slow deep breaths if you can."

It doesn't slow down.

At the hospital a commotion ensues as the doctor checks Brenda. Starts barking orders to staff. Two new people show up. Blood pressure cuffs, syringes, a drip, endless questions, a heart monitor. Then, thankfully, Brenda's heart slows down and mine starts back up again.

This repeats itself for several months until a diagnosis. A solution is offered. Edmonton heart specialists will burn extra or overactive muscles around the heart. The surgery will take five hours.

Garry, Karen, Jody, and I are all there to escort her stretcher ride up to surgery and to give her a thumbs up as they wheel her in and close the doors. I can't hold on any longer. I burst into tears. Thankfully, everything goes well that day. Two months later, we are back for a second surgery. They didn't burn enough away. After another five intense hours of pacing, no food and barely able to drink water, Brenda's heart problem is finally corrected.

Then there's the huge amount of time I spend, with my closest and dearest friend Aline, after the sudden and unexpected loss of her husband and soul mate. I often stay with her to help and support in whatever way she needs, as she travels through the unruly stages of grief that throw people into a discombobulated world. My heart aches for, and with her.

In the midst of all this, I am making plans and working towards the dream of opening a self-help/metaphysical bookstore/coffee shop combination to transition to once FCSS closes its doors.

I christen my store Prana, meaning, breath, life, and vitality of spirit. The dream is to offer people of like mind a place where they can come together, to share, discuss, learn, and spend time in a calm, relaxing, nourishing place to be. I stock my store with books, spiritual card decks, stones, crystals, candles, incense, rain sticks, music, and other various gifts to enhance meditation and a deepening of mind and soul.

The store has an office in the back where I continue to do counselling with clients. I absolutely love my work and watching how the store evolves from one day to the other. When I am not busy with things to do at the store, I keep myself busy with correspondence studies of spiritual mind classes with the minister from the Center for Spiritual Living in Edmonton, and enjoy deepening my spiritual side.

Then one day, I get the news. The landlord walks into my store, grabs a coffee and asks me to sit down.

"There's something I need to tell you. I've just signed the papers and closed on a deal. I've sold the property to the bank that is looking for a building site. I wanted you to hear from me. You will have to be out in three months."

I am devastated. My dream has been less than a year in the making.

September 20/95

I worked hard to make "Prana" happen. I'm proud of what I've created. I've enjoyed building a safe and warm receiving place for people to gather, share, read a book, write in their journal, and to meet and discuss what is going on in their lives. I've watched the place evolve and become what it is. This week I knocked on almost every door in town trying to find another place to rent. There's nothing. Absolutely nothing.

I constantly remind myself to breathe deeply, to flow with the changes and move on - that when one door closes another will open but it's easier said than done and often I find myself asking, *"What happens now?"*

Dear One:

There is a lot going on in my life and I can handle most of it but I am in bad need of some guidance when it comes to my relationships. I don't know if I should walk, run, not move, move slowly, or move ahead in full force.

It's not easy living the life I am living now. It's as if I'm standing on a pair of skis heading in opposite directions.

There's a lot of confusion within me. Not about my truth or about being with a woman. Things are clear that way.

What I'm confused about is what to do. How do I live my need to live in truth and how can I ever satisfy this thirst and hunger for Oneness if I am not one with myself?

Please guide me to make the choice to move forward and if it means to walk away then to be able to do so coming from a place of love.

Lou

Chapter 37

Justification or Authenticity

The concept of truth is as universal as the many different sizes and shapes we come in, but my individual truth is as specific as my thumbprint.

I tried to justify the affair with Madison knowing that what Garry and I once shared had ended a long time before Madison came into the picture and by telling myself that because I was with a woman, I was not really being unfaithful.

As the reality of my unrelenting need to live in truth becomes stronger and stronger, I know I can't continue living this way. It isn't fair to Madison, to Garry, or to me. I have discovered and accepted my sexuality, and it is becoming clear to me that I can't continue to live this truth in a deceitful way. My life has to change, and I am the only one who can make those changes happen.

I tell Madison I can no longer live my life with a foot in two different worlds and that I've decided to make changes that will allow me to live my truth, but I have to tell her several times before she realizes I am serious. We talk on the phone a few times after that, but our conversations are rather stilted and always end in an argument, misunderstandings or hurt feelings erupting from somewhere. She does not seem to understand my decision and many times I am too emotionally and psychologically taxed and drained to try to explain.

My days are a tangled mess of stress with a roller coaster of emotions as I not only prepare to leave my marriage, but also try to support and be there for my girls through what each of them are living in their own lives. Karen is discovering her chosen field of work is not right for her, Jody is about to graduate from college and Brenda is trying to adjust to city life, find a job and struggling to find her place in the world. Between being there as much as I possibly can for my girls and taking steps to move out of my twenty-three year marriage, my plate is more than full, and the more I talk to Madison about leaving Garry and the steps I am taking in that direction, the more she pulls away from me.

I am ready to move forward with my truth while she is not. Maybe she is full of fear. Maybe she can't see a way out of her marriage. Maybe, like me, she doesn't want to hurt anyone. Maybe she doesn't think she is strong enough to make that choice or still loves him, or maybe she has never trusted or understood how much I really love her, but the end result is, I know I can no longer stay where I am.

As I sit back and look at my life, I see all the duality.

There are times when I so desperately want to talk to someone about what I am living and have lived as a result of my relationship with Madison, but apart from Emily, I have no one to talk to. Confidentiality is sacred and Madison is not ready to be known even if I am.

The dilemmas of our truths intertwine, send me digging deeper into the tunnel of silence and once more I swallow my words to protect another.

Now I avoid those I am close to so I won't have to lie. I also fear for myself. I fear what will be the result if I speak up and say I had an affair with a woman. More losses I am not strong enough to deal with. It has taken me so long to form close, caring relationships, and I fear how it will threaten the very thing I treasure.

I question which of my friendships will still be there. But I realize there is no choice. I can't, nor do I want, to pretend, hide, or play games. I have to be true regardless. There is no turning back.

Dear One:

I don't want to lose my friends, yet how can I consider myself a true friend when I allow others to only see certain aspects of me, and I hide the ones I fear they will frown upon?

I can no longer present a persona that I believe will slide gently and pleasantly into other people's world. I want authenticity and integrity. I want to be me, totally and completely me and that's what I have to do even if it means others walk away.

Mark Nepo says, "Authenticity, the experience of truth, is our richest food. Without it we will freeze to death."

I need this food. I need to be One with and to live in warmth.

Lou

Chapter 38

Learnings

When I come to a crossroad, I hear a voice that asks, "What would love do?" And from there, I move forward accordingly.

Even if the girls had suspected it wasn't going well between Garry and me and had spoken about us amongst each other, when the reality of my words sunk in, they were shocked.

On my five hour trip to Edmonton to meet with each of the girls I can barely get enough air into my lungs. I need to find the courage to speak my truth no matter how hard it is. I ask for love and compassion to guide my words.

Yesterday I almost cancelled going to Edmonton. I was going to stay in my marriage with their father because I couldn't bring myself to break their hearts. This morning, I know I need to tell them in person. Tomorrow I will travel back home and tell Garry that I've talked to the girls.

We cry together, the girls and I. I try to reassure them Garry and I will still come together for Christmas and other important occasions, and that those kinds of things will remain the same, but we all know that even though no one has died, dreams have died, and yes, things will be different.

I want to wave a magic wand to erase their pain. I ache for them but in some strange way, I wonder if they feel a sense of relief no longer being in the unknown while suspecting there's something wrong.

That evening is bittersweet for me but I can breathe easier and the tightness that was squeezing my heart is a little less painful having spoken the words.

I know that people need time to adjust to the changes transition brings. My pulling away and stepping out of the life I have known for twenty-three years is certainly no exception to the rule. I am filled with questions, doubts, and fears of how my life will unfold. The right choice isn't always the easiest choice.

The hardest part about leaving is witnessing how everyone has to make adjustments in their lives because of the decision I've made. It makes me realize that as long as we live and breathe, our life affects other people's lives in some way. This makes me want to reach even deeper in my quest for *Oneness* in my life.

During the next seven to ten days I break down many times and shed many tears. Saying goodbye to friends and attending my last journaling group, and tying up loose ends leaves a lump the size of an orange sitting in my throat.

Once things are looked after, as best as I can for now, still exhausted and drained from the high stress level of the past month, I get on the road and drive the twelve hours it takes me to go to Kelowna, BC where my parents and my two sisters live. For months I concentrated all my effort and energy on leaving my home, my marriage, my friends, and right now I don't have any energy left to figure out the future. I can only rely on faith that I will somehow get back on my feet again.

When I arrive in Kelowna my sister Lucie says, "Mom is shocked that you have left Garry. She doesn't understand and thinks you shouldn't have left."

"Well, that doesn't surprise me."

"She didn't tell Dad yet. She said she doesn't know if she should. That maybe it's best not to tell him."

"Ya, somehow that doesn't surprise me. Mom believes that for-better-or-for-worse is a rule that should never be broken and this is the second time I break that rule. Dad avoids emotions by drinking himself into oblivion."

I know I can't live my life for other people or because of what they will think, say, or do. I can't take responsibility for this but my convictions are shaken when I am accused of disrupting everyone's life over and over again; drop by drop my strength leaks out like a drippy faucet, and once more I crumble inside.

For a while, I am either in tears or on the verge. My journal sits on the coffee table gathering dust. I don't want to feel the shitty horrible pain, the confusion, and the hopelessness that threatens to walk away with my sanity. I can only allow little bits of pain to come through at a time; otherwise, I feel I will go over the edge. There are moments when I feel doomed if I follow my heart and doomed if I don't.

The day after my arrival in Kelowna, I go stay at my sister's condo at Big White Ski Resort. With ski season over, the only people in the village are a few construction workers and cleanup crews. I have no phone and no contact with anyone. I am completely alone.

I expect my time alone in my own space to be good, but the call from Garry I received at my sister's house the night before I came to Big White has thrown me into a tizzy. A blanket of guilt weighs me down. What he says my decision to leave is doing to the girls is a high price to pay. I can't go back to my marriage like he asked. Just the thought of doing that squeezes the air out of my lungs.

I want to curl up in the corner and let the pain take me. I don't know how to handle what is happening, and I don't feel I have the strength to cope. I am the bad one, the spoiled one, the one who caused everyone pain. They see Garry destroyed by my choices. They do not see I needed to save me.

He was protected by my silence. I couldn't share with anyone about the joy of Madison and I didn't talk about how alone I felt in a lifeless marriage. I have kept how I felt to myself. Now I'm on top a mountain, feeling the pain, the guilt and the confusion rip me apart.

The first couple of nights are rough. On the third morning I wake up, look around outside and shift into a state of gratitude. I slept until nine, the longest I've slept in a very long time. Being up at Big White, in May when there's no one around is the best time to be here. It's beautiful and peaceful. Right now, the sun is beaming through the window and the knowledge that the next two days are mine to do what I want is a huge relief from the stress I've been under. I need this time and space. I'm grateful for the opportunity to sit, listen to music and allow my nerves to unravel.

Things look brighter this morning but I realize I've barely eaten. Food tastes like sawdust and my stomach feels like something foreign crawled inside. I'm worried about what comes next. Everyone sees me as the strong one, the one who doesn't hurt but that's because I'm far away and they can't see me right now.

They don't see what it has been like for me, how the decision I made to leave is not one I made lightly, what I had to let go of, how difficult it is now, the worry of not knowing where I'm going from here, if I'll find a job, when, or how I'll live. I know I play a big role in this with my brave front and my silence.

I also know I can't stay here and lick my wounds forever. I have to look for a place to start over.

Tomorrow, I will get on the road and try to find a place to call home again.

May 21/98

I've been on the road for five days now. I am rootless. I wander aimlessly without ties to a home or a community and it's getting to me. I don't know what to do. I want a place to call my own. Every time I sit down to write I cry.

I'm tired of looking, tired of driving, tired of living out of my car. Where the hell will I settle? I don't have a home. Don't have work. I can feel my energy and enthusiasm drain from me. I'm tired of the unknown. I miss my friends. There was no other road to choose.

May 24/98

I've had a lot of hard days but my life is my own. My spirit feels free. I've been on the road most of the time, always moving from one place to another.

May 26/98

A bitch of a day. Draining. Exhausting. I got a letter from my daughter Karen this morning, and it sent me over the edge for a while. She wants to know more about what happened between Garry and me. I'm okay with that, but her way of saying things is straight from the hip. There's no beating around the bush, that's for sure, but at least one knows where one stands with her. I have to admire that.

May 27/98

Finally! I found an apartment to move into. Soon. Soon, I'll have a home in Spruce Grove.

I wrote in my journal today, June 4th, about the gratitude I feel that it is my last day sleeping at someone else's house in someone else's bed. The move that I was beginning to doubt would ever happen is happening tomorrow. I don't have a bed, a dresser, a kitchen table, a toaster, a microwave or a TV. I don't have much of anything, but I have my computer and boxes and boxes of my books that I brought with me when I left the farm.

It doesn't take long for me to settle in and I don't lose any time to start pounding the pavement handing out resumes and cover letters. Evenings, I write and read.

A week after moving into my apartment, I get a call from my mom in Kelowna. She asks how I am doing and how I am feeling and, before I have a chance to respond, quickly adds, "Dad knows nothing about you. Doesn't even know I'm calling you right now."

Nothing has changed. The secrecy continues and Dad has to be protected at all costs. The game is always to pretend. It is much easier for her to cope that way.

Once more, I realize I have to accept who they are. Unless I have walked in their shoes, I only have a limited knowledge of what went on for them. Besides, if I want others to accept where I am, I have to learn to accept others where they are and love them for who they are.

I realize that as much as I want to live alone, I often feel very lonely. Had I stayed in the area where I lived most of my life it would have been easier. I live closer to my girls but I don't want to start relying on them. They have their lives to live. I have to form my own.

I keep telling myself I need to be patient. I need to trust that things will work out. I am happy now. I go to sleep at night content and I wake up looking forward to the days ahead. My heart no longer feels heavy and resentment is no longer knocking at my door. I am on my way to living truth.

I allow myself to live authentically through writing, crying, bleeding on the page. This is part of the vision of the five-year-old, to allow people to see the true me so others can feel free.

Dear One:

Every day I'm learning.

Every day I realize we need to become who we are rather than who we became.

Every day I see the importance of continually searching for our truth.

Every day I learn about how we need to trust, to be open, to be vulnerable and to find ways to walk our talk; otherwise we risk missing what life is all about and getting to the end of it wishing: if only we would have.

Every day I become aware of how we need to believe in the goodness of people including our own.

Every day I feel our need as people to be seen, to be heard, to be recognized and loved for who we are.

Every day I'm learning.

As someone so eloquently said and I've discovered, "Within my sensitivity lies my strength."

I have worked through and tackled head on the pain, fear, and all the other emotions that came hurtling at me. Looking back at the me of ten years ago, I am grateful for my journey

I just needed to say that.

Lou

PS: The Oneness, connection and love – its coming! Right?

Chapter 39

Coming Into Truth

Truth pulls me forward and calls my name.

She calls to say she is on her way back from a trip to Vancouver and asks if I can pick her up at the airport. I tell her I will. We spend a few hours together catching up on how things are going in each our own worlds, and at first things are going fine. Then, all of a sudden, things go awry. Anger, hurt, questioning words and accusations fly in my direction, and I am once more caught in a profusion of words I am no match for. It is eleven at night when she asks to be driven to the airport to catch the next flight home. I feel the walls of self-protection go up around my heart and tell her I will go start the car.

I coat myself with a thick skin of indifference. When we get to the airport, I am expressionless; nothing penetrates the thickness of my walls. My goodbye is brief. Deadpan. Erecting walls is something I am familiar with - it's called protecting, keeping hurt at bay, knowing that if one more ounce of hurt penetrates my shield of indifference I will go under. My heart is broken but I know I cannot travel this road again. I remain calm, my face blank. Her words have sliced through me, and I am like a baby seal, defenseless against the attack. I can't find the strength to fight back.

"I am the victim," she said.

I was destroying her. Causing her hurt and betraying her once more. The drama mounted with me as the villain, the deceitful one, the one with no consideration for her or how she felt.

It was yet another scene added to the many; only this time it was different. This time it broke me and I shut down. Never had I loved so deeply, and never had I felt so misunderstood.

When love reached her she turned and ran. Each time she ran, she took a piece of me with her.

There's nothing left.

I can no longer reach out. This time I know it is goodbye.

All the hard work I have done and do with Emily to be able to express myself has made absolutely no difference with Madison. Is it better if I stay clear of relationships all together? I have struggled to speak from my heart and since Kevin has died, I have tried so hard and I thought it was better, but have I been kidding myself? At a time when it is most crucial, I have failed.

I feel like I have been thrown off my horse, yet I know I am more rooted and more grounded than ever before. I know this relationship has allowed me to recognize truth and to welcome it into my life. The relationship with Madison, and everything it brought to me, is an immeasurable gift and I would not change this.

Following my own path and claiming my sexual identity isn't going to be easy but at least it's a true path that feels right for me.

Choosing to live my truth will complicate my life and other's lives, but turning my back on my truth will be worse than following it.

How can I be true to another if I cannot be true to myself?

I have arrived at my truth. Now I need to learn how to wear it.

Dear One:

I'm feeling pretty raw right now. It all seems so stupid to me. Why can't love just be LOVE? Why does love have restrictions, rules, and boundaries? Why is love something that has to fit within a prescribed framework? Who says that there is only one right way of loving people?

We spend a whole bloody lifetime trying to adjust to the framework, giving up pieces of ourselves, becoming someone other than who we feel we are, and all the time we complain and feel that there must be more to life. It's not easy living the life I have been living with a foot in two different worlds. I have been so confused and the loyal part of me has felt ill.

Every day since I got involved with Madison, I've tortured myself with the question of what to do with the need to share my life with a woman, combined with the reality I was in of sharing my life with a man.

There is nothing more beautiful or more natural to me than to love a woman. It feels right. So completely right. It's hard to understand how I didn't welcome this part of me before. It's hard to realize that so much of my life has been about living within other people's script.

Like Andre Gide said; "It is better to be hated for what you are than loved for what you are not."

I agree.

Lou

PART THREE

Chapter 40

Stand By Me

Vulnerability makes me human.

In the 10 years I worked at FCSS. I developed close and dear relationships with a few women, sharing the details of our lives in deeply connected ways.

My friends and I philosophize and analyze, we laugh and we cry, we question and we share about ourselves and our individual journeys. I love every minute of it, but because of the nature of my work, part of me remains guarded in what I share about myself, especially when it implicates someone else.

After I leave my position at FCSS and open my self-help bookstore, I feel freer to talk about what is going on for me on a personal level and I share bits and pieces of the inner turmoil I am in, but again, I remain guarded to protect others.

Much later, it becomes public knowledge that I've walked away from my twenty-three year marriage. When I become involved with a woman, people are shocked, resentful, betrayed, and even hurt that I haven't shared with them. Then there are two other groups, the ones who know and empathize with me and the ones who need a new item to gossip about. Small town gossip spreads like grass fires pushed by gale force winds. Like a fire, gossip leaves destruction behind but rarely truth and never the whole story.

I am surprised. There are people who I think will always be there, no matter what, who disengage and pull away, while others, who I don't expect will be there, want to be.

One person who doesn't abandon my ship is Andree. Although I've known Andree since her divorce through my work at FCSS, it isn't until I leave my employment that she becomes a bigger part of my life. Opposite of the confusion with Madison, everything is straightforward, no beating around the bush or chasing a monkey up a tree. I know what Andree feels, what is going on for her and why. She says what she means and means what she says. Genuine. Real. Uncomplicated. There are no mind games. This makes sense to me.

Andree, is a down-to-earth, no frills kind of person. She thrives on the gathering of friends and family around her kitchen table for a home-cooked meal and some hearty discussions. This kind of uncomplicated way of relating with people, and a simplistic lifestyle combined with ample time in nature feeds her soul and makes her day. I find myself relaxed and at ease in her company.

Both Andree and I exited the high school dance floor and walked into marriages we were unprepared for. She had four children, three boys and one girl and I had four children, one boy and three girls. She now enters my journal.

July 20/97

I just remembered the dream I had last night and it stopped me from writing in mid-sentence. For a minute, I almost thought it was real. I was with Andree for a weekend. We were spending time together and we became more intimate than usual in our interaction with each other, and it all happened so very naturally.

The dream feels real. I wonder if she's ever had any feelings like that towards another woman, or maybe even towards me? She's never indicated that but I'm almost sure she has. It's just a feeling I have. I don't know why.

August 7/97

Andree still occupies my thoughts. Does she have thoughts about me occupying her mind I wonder? I never experienced these feelings with other friends. I think the reason I feel this with Andree is because the same feelings live within her. Why can't we just come out with it instead of acting like a couple of teenagers who have no idea what to do with what they feel? Actually, maybe I should just blurt it all out. If she's feeling the same thing, it will be an opportunity for her to come out with it, too. Or maybe she's in a place like I was and she never had the chance to explore the possibility of having a relationship with a woman. At least that's not where the doubt is for me. Maybe that's what I need to share with her.

August 24/97

I had another one of those dreams about Andree last night and again it all feels so normal. There is no shame, no judgment or feelings of living anything wrong. It just is what it is. But for now it's nothing more than me dreaming.

I returned Andree's call. She might come and visit me today while I'm camped at the lake. I wonder what she thinks. Was she shocked when I told her I had an affair with a woman? She didn't seem to be, but maybe she's thought about it more, and she'd like to talk about it now.

She's the one who called yesterday to say she might come to join me. I suspect she's had similar thoughts. Maybe she's never acted on them, but I'm almost positive those thoughts are there as much as they are for me. I hope she comes. I like being with her. It's so natural, so uncomplicated, so easy and she's such a beautiful woman with a big heart. Besides, we enjoy good conversation, a good laugh, nature and each other's company. So why not give each other that since both of us seem to be searching for and seeking the same thing.

I wonder if she sees it as a search for *Oneness* like I often do? I think so. Especially times like when we are both laying on the picnic table searching for the different constellations in the sky, sharing how our adult children are navigating life, what our views are about relationships, or the different struggles and rewards of staying true to ourselves.

Andree has a contract delivering the Edmonton Sun newspaper to businesses. The job requires that she travels six hundred twenty-five kilometers a day and sometimes I go with her to help her do her run. Not that I can help all that much but we enjoy the opportunity to chat in the confined space of a vehicle while traveling 625 km together under a moonlit sky. Even the sound of an owl hooting while sitting in her pickup truck on the side of the road in the middle of nowhere waiting for her paper bundles to arrive, can keep us busy sharing all kinds of stories with each other.

Other times we go out for supper or to an occasional movie, and a couple of times, we go to Edmonton to do some shopping and see a play. Sometimes we spend time together at the lake when I go there with the motor home or I join her when she is staying at her friend's cabin.

We walk, read, talk, play cards, and have a good time just being out in nature watching the squirrels by day and the stars by night. We don't see each other all the time, but when we do it is nurturing and relaxing, and we come away feeling we thoroughly enjoyed each other's company.

Later, in May of 1998, after I leave my marriage and the area where I've lived for almost all my life, the friendship I share with Andree and my other friends, Joce and Joyce continue to be a huge support for me.

I borrow my brother's pick-up truck, load my books and my few belongings, and drive to Edmonton where I put them in storage until I figure out where I will settle and live. Then I drive back to my brother's to pick up my car. From there I start what ends up being close to a two-month search for a possible place to settle, find work, and start a new life. After almost two months of travelling and investigating and not being any further ahead, I start to lose hope.

When tired and weary from couch surfing and trying to find work, I decide to rent an apartment in a place on the outskirts of Edmonton called Spruce Grove. It is close to, yet far enough from where my daughters live so I won't be involved in their day to day lives. I desperately need a place to hang my hat and an address where people can reach me when I apply for work. I am certain that once I have a place to call home and I hit the pavement with a mountain of resumes, I will find a job. I am wrong. It doesn't work that way.

The difficulty in getting a job in a place where nobody knows me is it doesn't matter how honest or dedicated I am, what my work ethics are, or what values I hold. Unless my resume stands out from the four hundred others, my character and background mean nothing. In all the applications I hand out, not one interview comes my way.

My funds are running low. With no work in sight, I wonder what to do next. Do I give my notice to leave my apartment because I have no money to cover next month's rent? Do I take a risk and hope I'll have a job and enough money put together by the first of the month? If I leave, where do I store my belongings and where do I go? Live where? Do what?

My options are few. I give my notice to vacate my apartment. My supply of rice and bread looks rather lonely sitting on a shelf all by itself in a huge cupboard and my cash funds have dwindled to the double digits. I have a small RRSP (Registered Retirement Savings Plan) that I have paid into while working at Family and Community Support Services for ten years, but I will lose a good chunk of it if I cash it in early. I have to hang on as long as I can.

Some nights my mind spins out of control and as much as I am against mind-numbing things like TV and anxiety pills, I am almost tempted to go there. I want to escape. I want to obliterate the worry and stop my mind from jumping on the hamster wheel. I tell myself to trust that everything will be fine, but the evidence in front of me makes me wonder what being fine will look like, and when it will come about.

Along with the financial worry, the emotional stuff jumps into the pot and rears its ugly head. There are evenings when I weep uncontrollably, and pace around my living room floor like a circling dog. Questions swirl around in a whirlwind in my head. Should I disregard what is important to me for the sake of what others want? Have I screwed up everyone's life with the decisions I have made? Have I done the right thing? Made the right choices?

For the next two days, I cry and sob continuously. I can't stop. I sit on my living room floor and rock myself in place with my hands hugging my shoulders and my chin resting on my chest.

Then, as if meant to be, Joce, Andree and Emily call to check on me to make sure I haven't, in a moment of desperation, thrown myself over the balcony. I don't tell them how bad things are. I am grateful to hear their voices and reassured and grounded by their down-to-earth approach and response to things. It helps to remind me of my strength and that no matter what, I am not alone. That thought brings comfort and I ask myself if this too is part of the *Oneness* I seek.

Their calls and words of encouragement and support help me snap out of the self-inflicted guilt stupor and make me realize I have to shift my energy. I have no other choice.

Come morning, I force myself out of bed, jump into my pants and take off for a thirty-five minute power walk down the trails. Returning, I put my last two pieces of bread to toast in the oven (no toaster), eat, shower and hum to myself in order to keep the guilt and worry roaming around in my psyche at bay. I fight to push away the demons telling me I have messed up a lot of people's lives. I have to be vigilant. It would be easy to let myself slip into a lethargic state of sleep and isolation, so I fight to stay above water like a cat trying to claw its way out of a bathtub.

July 20/98

It's been three months since I left home and moved to Spruce Grove. Emotionally things are going a bit better. The financial struggle continues.

So far, out of all the people I have known, Andree is the only one who, like me, often had to rely on her own steam to move ahead in this world. We step into our britches. We have to.

With people like Andree and Joce, I know where they stand. They make their own decisions and are not afraid to speak their minds. They do their own thing, speak their mind, and I do the same. It's a model that works well for me.

This morning Andree returned my call and said she's found someone to do her run. Then she asked if it was okay if she came for a visit. I'm waiting for her arrival now. It's a good thing she's coming or I'd be crying my eyes out again. The phone calls and letters of support and encouragement from her, Joce and Emily have kept me from weaving my bed sheets into a hangman's noose.

The correspondence and calls from Garry don't hold promise of anything getting settled anytime soon. Every day I watch my financial situation deteriorate. I'm down to $125 and I need to make this money last. The only thing I have to go on after that is trust.

My days are focused on looking for work, but so far nothing has materialized and the funds keep dwindling. I'm grateful Karen invited me to stay for supper last night. Rice again otherwise. The girls have no idea. It's not their place to worry about me.

Since Andree called to confirm she's coming to spend a week, it's certainly lifted my spirit. I know Andree's been there before, wondering how to make whatever food is left stretch into another day, another week or until the end of the month. She will understand. Still, I am humbled.

I take a few more books to the secondhand bookstore. It takes me a while to figure out which ones I can part with. I need enough cash to buy bread and butter so Andree and I can make toast.

The comfort and the life her company brings me when faith in myself is hanging by a thread, does wonders. There is no measure for that kind of friendship and I know no amount of money can buy what a friend brings.

Dear One:

Selfish. Is it a bad word? Is it something to shy from? Or, is it something we need to embrace as a necessary part of our lives? Can it also be self-care? Self-preservation?

Sometimes I wonder which is harder, making decisions to look after our own needs or ignoring them completely.

Selfless giving is honorable but giving at the cost of losing our self and who we are... who says that is healthy or honorable?

A healthy self-love is not only okay but absolutely necessary.

If someone else's needs are always defining who I am, I live my life as a shadow, a pantomime with no voice of my own. Unless I can honor and respect who I am, how can I honor and respect someone else? Unless I can give to myself, how can I give to another? Unless I honor my truth, how can I guide others to live theirs? I can't give what I don't have.

If I stand by me then I'll have the strength to stand by others. Right?

Lou

PS: I'm learning. Oneness doesn't come from a place of will. It comes from a place of heart. I'm learning this from the connection I feel with friends like Emily, Joce, Andree and a few others who stand by me. All I can do right now is to remain open to the learning.

Chapter 41

Living from the Heart

Let me tell about the many colors of my truth. Then you will tell me of yours and our souls will have touched the tapestry of who we are.

Then there was the evening that turned into a weekend that turned into a lifetime that has led to now.

I am aware that the moves I make when she comes to visit me will change everything. I'm not talking about walking from the corner store to the post office. I'm talking about inviting her to lie down next to me on the futon by the patio door so we can listen to the rumble of the thunder and watch the lightning crisscross the dark evening sky. It doesn't take long before the passion and fury of the storm outside transposes and ignites our bodies inside.

I know that once I cross over from a friendship into the realm of a physical relationship that things will not and cannot, remain the same. Intentionally or not, once boundaries melt away in our mutual attraction for each other, things change. I am taking a risk. Our relationship will either get more involved or we will be forced to say goodbye. But, just like knowing there's a storm outside doesn't make the storm stop – neither does knowing that things will change make us stop from giving in to riding the waves of heat and passion that match the fury of the storm.

Already things are more complicated. After last week and what transpired between us, I am filled with a strange mixture of excitement and fear. There's the possibility of experiencing a deep meaningful connection and being One with another and the fear of losing everything including a long and dear friendship.

I keep giving my head a shake and telling myself to push thoughts of last week and everything else out of my mind when right now I don't even know where I will live or how. I need to stay focused on the present moment to put one foot in front of the other and try to hang on to the hope that somehow everything will work itself out.

The words truth and trust flash in front of my eyes and follow me around like a puppy at my heels. Things happened fast and I worry that what Andree lived and expressed over the week we had together is more about being with a woman for the first time than it is about being with me. I know how exciting and freeing it feels to experience being in the "right place" and how powerful and seductive that can be but this is totally new to her.

I am also concerned that Andree did not have time to grasp the extent of what it means to live in a same-sex relationship. I have a pretty good idea of how beautiful, as well as how difficult, it can be.

I am excited but I also feel like I am about to go white water rafting on a raging river with no idea of how to handle the situation. I chastise myself. Why have I allowed myself to get involved so quickly, so deeply and to complicate things even further?

I hope we can play it cool, go back to being friends, but something tells me we would be kidding ourselves and neither one of us is willing to play games anymore. It is part of a past life we're not willing to go back to but my loving feelings are laced with fear. I'm petrified of hurting others and myself again. The only thing that reassures me is our solid friendship.

Already I have shared with Andree things I have never shared with anyone else before. It is easy. It feels good. And when we're apart, I miss her and want her back in my life.

I go for a walk to fight the loneliness and browse stores looking for something to send her to let her know I miss her. I see things I can't afford. I go back home feeling lost and tearful, and when I reach for a glass in the cupboard, I discover she has tucked a hundred dollar bill in the corner - money which she likely needs as much as, if not more than I do.

For two weeks following Andree's visit I hand out resume after resume still hanging on to the hope, but there are no jobs. If there are any, the ton of resumes I sent out is not producing a single one. I have no money to pay next month's rent so I pack my things and arrange to vacate my apartment.

September 1/98

So much is happening all at once in my life that I don't even have time to write about it all. Nothing but brief entries find their way into my journal.

I'm enjoying my stay at Andree's right now. I made the drive to her place yesterday. I know I can't stay long. I have to move on, but she has offered me to stay while I figure things out.

No home, no job, no plan of action. I'm tired of the uncertainty but I'm happy to have choices. I'm less desperate now than when I was in a marriage I felt suffocated in.

September 3/98

It's been nice here at Andree's. Really nice. Sometimes I panic when I realize how fast things have evolved between us and sometimes I try to run but I don't run far.

As hard and as trying as the last four months have been, I can say it's been a long time since I have been this happy. I don't live under the same heaviness that lingered like a fog that wouldn't lift.

I may not have a clear pathway to a destination but at least I can breathe. There's a lot of uncertainty and an undefined future ahead of me, but I feel a lot of progress in living who I am. That feels damn good.

September 5/98

I'm sitting in my car at the park outside of town desperately trying to reach Andree on my cell phone. I was heading back to the Edmonton area after having said goodbye to her, but I put the brakes on. I realize I can't leave. At least that much has become clear to me. As crazy as it may sound, I can't make myself take the highway back... back to where? To an apartment I don't have? To a non-existent job? What am I going to?

I close my eyes, center myself, and ask: What is it I want? What does my heart tell me? What would love do right now? And the answer I hear is: Chase the fear. Follow your heart. This is part of the Oneness you seek.

September 6/98

Such a good feeling to be doing what I want rather than what I feel I should be doing. I turned my car around and headed back to

Andree's yesterday. The more time I spend with her, the more I realize how very easy and natural it is. There's nothing like being true, being real.

I say what I feel, I ask for what I want and need, I allow myself to hurt, to cry and to love openly - that in itself surpasses anything I ever imagined. There is no need to say, "Will the real me please stand up?" The real me is standing up.

There's no doubt about it, 1998 has been and continues to be a tremendous year of learning and transformation. After I left my marriage in April and I embarked on a different journey into a new life. It feels as if I've entered some kind of time warp with no beginning, no middle, no end and no defining points. It has been one continuous string of intense living experiences - often scary, but also deep, alive, and true.

There are times when I'd like to stop the merry-go-round from turning so I could have a breather. A moment now and then to process, assimilate and learn from the events that whiz by my head like a hummingbird in flight. I want to holler, "Whoa slow down, let me catch my breath." Yet I don't want to live any other way.

Since Andree has become a bigger part of my life, things feel wonderful. My mind tells me I am crazy to let this happen when things are such a mess in both of our lives, but my heart tells me nothing has ever been better.

Andree has a hard time keeping up with her job because of her health but it is the only way she can keep up with her mortgage. I am out of house and home, and still looking for work. We are both on very shaky ground in the physical world, but in the world of relationships, we feel solid and grounded. How can we not follow what our heart tells us.

We try to figure out what our options are and together we come up with the town of Hinton to try to make a go of it together. Trees, mountains, lakes, streams all say home, plus I've heard someone is looking for a short term house sitter. It's perfect! I can start looking for work and line up an apartment for us. Andree will join me and start looking for work once I've found us a place to move to.

I set out for Hinton thinking I will see Andree again in about a month or so. Once I get to the house I am looking after, I start handing out resumes and the very next day I get a call and I'm told I can start right away. It's only a cleaning job and its minimum wage, but minimum wage is better than no wage and for that I'm grateful. I agree to take it and to start the next day but I keep looking for a better paying job and an apartment for us. I've been at my job for a week when I get a phone call.

"Hello"

"Hi Annette, this is Dale, Andree asked me to give you a call."

I get that sick feeling in the pit of my stomach again and I can feel my heart thump against my chest.

"She said you'd be worried about her if you didn't hear and she can't call. She asked me to. She's in the hospital. Don't worry. She's okay. She'll be fine."

My voice shakes. "When did she go in? Why? What happened?"

Dale continues, "She wasn't feeling well so I told her to come to emergency, and they've admitted her. They think maybe a heart attack. They're not sure. They're doing tests. Keeping her quiet. She said, don't worry. She'll call soon."

I thank Dale, hang up, think for five minutes and go speak to my boss. I explain, I ask for a week to go see Andree even though I just started my job.

As I drive back to Falher, I think about Andree's health giving out on her and how as a result, decisions have been made for her now. It's clear she will have to give up her contract. My mind races, long recovery time, no health benefits, no income, house payments and I can't help, plus I'm going through a difficult divorce which is about as pleasant as wading through quicksand or picking scabs off a wound.

Still, I remain optimistic. Something will work out and together, we'll pull through.

I can't believe that Spirit, or whatever greater force is out there that's brought us together to share this experience, would suddenly decide to drop us like a hot potato. I have faith that this greater force will show me what steps to take any time now.

I know and I believe that the light bulb will go on when I flip the switch on the wall even if I don't see how it happens. I also believe in what we've found with each other even if I can't quite see how it's all going to work out right now.

This is the first relationship I've been in where I don't feel I have to keep a part of me hidden behind the curtain waiting to see if it is safe to come to center stage. I am not giving that up.

The changes in Andree's health cause things to unfold much quicker than we anticipated. It's not what we had in mind but I know I have to find a way to make it work.

It isn't long before I land, not the best, but at least a better paying full-time job, and I am able to rent an apartment for both of us to move into. The paycheck isn't big but it is enough to manage if we are careful. I go to work, Andree begins her journey to better health, and both of us begin our life together.

September 27/98

Today I shared a peaceful day with Andree surrounded by the beauty and magnificence of the Rockies. I feel connected and I am grateful for how rich my life is now. The importance of living each moment for what it is has become paramount to both of us.

What is most important in life, I have right now and that makes me one of the wealthiest persons in the world.

The present is what I need to be part of and that's really all there is. The past is over and done. I can't go back to reclaim or change it. The future is unknown, forever changing by what I make of today, and, the present moment is the place I choose to be.

I imagine there will be hoops to jump through living life as a gay woman, but this is where I need to be. I'm sad it took me until my late forties to get here. I have great respect for those who are clear about who they are, from the moment they're old enough to step into a pair of shoes. For me it has been a journey of discovery, courage and determination to never give up.

Welcoming, rather than denying, my love for a woman makes me feel alive. I'm living a total freedom of self with another where I can cry, sing, laugh, talk, be silent, or as loving and as passionate as I feel. No more hiding, shame, guilt, or embarrassment. There is only this moment with no need to escape. I am the energy and the power of a wild horse needing to run free on an open range. I allowed society, circumstances and the limits of my own mind to corral me. I've been kept in check by the saddle and rider on my back and the constant pulling and tugging of the reins. Not anymore.

I've ditched the rider, thrown the saddle, and spit out the bit. I trot around, ears perked, eyes darting, muscles flexed, as I gaze at the open fields and my heart beats with a sense of passion and possibility. The smell of the green grass and the feel of the wind see me through the challenges. I've never looked back since the sky lit up the night. This is what it is to be alive.

In Andree, I've found someone who dares to be true to who she is, and I am grateful she has chosen to share her life with mine no matter what unfolds or life presents us with. Like the trees that bare their leaves in the fall, we stand naked before each other and reveal the truth of who we are.

I am grateful to share my life with someone who believes in me, and believes in my passion for the written word. Someone who can sit with me in the silence, hand me my pen when I'm struggling for answers she knows I hold within. Someone who is not afraid to sit with me in my truth, my tears or my fears.

It is the constancy and solidity of this love that makes things like grocery shopping and dusting more bearable to do. And it's from this same place that I hold her close, make her laugh and let her know how special she is. It is from this place that I live in truth with her, travel with her through the mountains she loves and share bedtime stories with her. It is from this place that I put on my big boy shorts and chase down all the spiders or whatever else is threatening her.

I did not know her in the morning of my life, but I am full of gratitude that she has chosen to share the afternoon of her life with me.

Dear One:

I read somewhere that we don't choose love – love chooses us. I like that.

Life is completely different. I can't believe how quickly things have changed. A few months ago I wondered if I'd ever experience Oneness in relationship. Now I live this with Andree. What more can I possibly ask for? My heart is full and my life rich, not with monetary value but with what makes life worth living and valuable.

I've learned that opening the heart and living from the heart is where being One is born from.

Lou

Chapter 42

Lessons, Choices & Struggles

I have to be willing to enter the silence, the spaces between the thoughts that continually circle my monkey mind.

Whether I've chosen the path less traveled or the path less traveled has chosen me–it doesn't matter. It's where it's at for me.

I'm happier than a pilot on a first solo flight. At 46 I have a new lease on life living closer to truth and comfortable with who I am. I've stepped into a pair of shoes molded to my feet.

Over the past 10 years, I've learned more is not better, nor does it fill the holes and make a person happy. I've learned I can do without a lot of things but I cannot do without the emotional and mental well-being.

I've learned that earning money is important, but money is irrelevant if I don't have time or health. I've learned to be spontaneous, to live in the moment and to cherish each moment for the blessing and the gift that it holds.

I've learned that I don't want to leave this life saying, I wish I would have. When I leave, I want to be saying, I did it and I did it my way.

I've learned that the more things I let go of, the richer I become. I can be without a job status or title to define who I am but I cannot be without *Oneness*.

I've also learned a lot of things regarding choices. For one thing choices aren't always easy or to our liking, and for another thing even if it looks like we have a choice, it often doesn't feel like we do.

For instance, some people think I should have chosen a different path than I did, but in my heart, I know that there is no other choice.

When I chose to leave my first marriage, even though I had two small children, I left because I felt I had to. I didn't really have another choice.

When I held our dog in my arms while the vet administered the injection that would put her to sleep, I had to help her die with dignity. She deserved that and that was the choice.

When I kept secrets as a child, it was because I didn't know how to break the silence or to deal with the shame I felt and what it would do to my family. I could not see another choice.

When the doctors told me they had to disconnect the respirator from my fourteen-year old son because he was brain dead and there was nothing else they could do, I didn't have a choice.

When the doctors asked me if I could donate my son's organs, How could I not help save someone's life? I had to make that choice.

When I left my second marriage, others thought I should stay. When a person feels like they are dying inside, there is no other choice.

Right now, some people think I have a choice in the kind of lifestyle I live. Again, there is no other choice.

Another situation where I don't feel I have a choice right now is how painstakingly slow things are going in reaching a settlement with my divorce. If it was up to me this would have all been settled a long time ago. But do I have a choice?

February 22/99

Divorce lawyer, ex-husband, and settlement battles. I'm so damn tired. It's been ten months since I left and still nothing is settled, nothing has changed except a legal bill that keeps climbing higher and higher. I don't think I'm any further ahead with this than when I left. When and where will it all end? I don't know what to do with the anger.

I wanted to be nice, to be fair, but right now, I could skin him alive. Why avoid, delay, deny, ignore? Is he trying to wish it all away the way he wished the trouble in our marriage would go away?

After ten months of this, you would think we could just get on with things already!

I've twisted myself into a pretzel in order to survive, to fit into relationships or to follow the norms. I have contorted and distorted myself in order to love and be loved. Life is just too damn short.

If I poke far enough into anyone's problems, won't I find we are all trying to be loved, accepted without compromise from the moment we are born?

As a strong-willed child, I presented a brave front to protect the frightened, fragile spirit hiding inside.

When a child's boundaries are violated, it messes up their ability to define and stand in who they are. When my boundaries were violated, I became a shadow stretching in all directions, obscure, vague and undefined.

Out of fear I learned to conform which was not always a bad thing but often a limiting one. How might my life have evolved if empowered to be who I was rather than what people, family and society expected or wanted me to be.

Had I felt free enough to entertain the fantasies, feelings and urges that visited the confines of my body and psyche, had I not been so eager to please others, had I loved myself enough to live what was right for me. Would it have taken me as long to step into my shoes and dance my own dance?

I can't pinpoint exactly when or how but I know that through Emily's help, her relentless willingness to be there, and my perseverance to push through, I morphed into myself like a caterpillar coming out of its cocoon and now I am *One* with me.

A little while ago, I read a book called *"The Unimaginable Life"* by The Loggins, and I wrote a quote in my journal that says, "When we hide nothing we can give everything." Standing in our truth is challenging and I found it especially challenging when it could cause hurt to people I loved.

We think our secrets will make others run in the opposite direction, or is it more our fear of what others might say if we dare to speak?

Secrets have weighed me down and tangled me in a web of fear—fear of hurting others, of being hurt, of being judged, or being abandoned. I carried the weight of too many secrets far too long. I never want to feel like a prisoner behind self-erected walls again. Truth can hurt. It can also heal and set us free. I ask for the strength to never hide anything, so I can learn to give everything.

By May of 1999, Andree and I decide to leave Hinton, Alberta, and drive to the Okanagan in BC where we stay until March of 2000. When we leave, we are optimistic we will find work to keep us going until my divorce is settled, and with my share of the settlement, we hope to be able to get our own place. In the meantime, I have no other choice but to cash my RRSP in order to pay for rent and food until we find work.

Unfortunately, things often work better in our mind's eye than in actual practice. Again, jobs are hard to get. Andree manages to get a part-time job at a bingo hall and I find a part-time job at an open-air fruit market by Highway 97 where the locals on their way to real jobs, and a million tourists, whizz by me all day.

At summer's end, our seasonal work has run out, so we try our hand at picking grapes when fruit season comes along. It doesn't take long to discover this is a task better left to the younger more supple bodies, than two women in their fifties. Not being used to the intense heat of the Okanagan, and not having any experience picking fruits, results in not much money in our pocket by the end of the day, and every muscle in our bodies pleading with us not to go back, but we do anyway. By October we are at our wits end.

October 27/99

What can I do now? One month left. At the end of November, that's it. There won't be anything. My RRSP will have run out. What will we do then? There's nowhere else to draw from. I feel defeated. I was sure I could make it work and I can't

Dear One:

Why? Why do Andree and I, have to struggle to keep our head above water and food in our stomach and still not make it? We have been working like dogs for the past two days and we've made $140.

When I left my marriage, I was in a position where I no longer had to work, but I was slowly dying. Now, I am full of life but I can't provide a way for us to stay alive. Really? Does it have to be one or the other?

My heart breaks to see Andree absolutely worn right out. I don't want to see her sick the way she was last year. Right now we are both physically exhausted and in rough shape. We can't do this every day. I desperately want to find a way to earn a living that will be comfortable for both of us. That's all I ask. I can't bear to see her suffer like she is tonight. Please help me find a way.

It's been one challenge after another for the past two years. I am drained. There are times when I am tempted to crawl into a hole, curl into a ball, go to sleep and never wake up.

Answers. Do you have any? Hello? I don't hear you... But then, I probably wouldn't hear you even if you were answering... I'm that tired.

Have faith. Trust. Go for your dreams. Those are my words, my motto, but right now, I'm beginning to question if I've been pulling my own chain. The one thing I love doing is to write, and tonight, even pushing my pen across the page is too hard, I'm that tired.

I'm tired of the struggle. Tired of trying. Tired of battling. Just plain tired. I don't want to give up, but I don't know which way to turn. I hurt inside and out. I feel like I'm letting Andree down, letting my friends down, letting myself down. Is that what you want? Am I supposed to throw my arms up in the air and give up?

Well, I'm not going to! So there! I might not have a lot left but I'm going to dig a little further and find a way to hang on.

Lou

Chapter 43

Searching

If we're willing to listen and be attentive to it, there is a driving force that moves us towards truth that not only wants to, but needs to, live within us.

Without jobs and no promise of any with the BC economy, we packed up and left. For a while we were like gypsies.

Nov. 25/99

I got a call from my lawyer, Dawn. Finally it looks like an agreement has been reached with Garry and this divorce settlement will be over before Christmas.

I have agreed to receive the settlement in four different installments. Helpful for Garry, but this will make it harder for me to get on my feet. The first payment will disappear paying my sisters back for their loan covering my lawyer's retainer fees and the rest gobbled up by accumulated lawyer costs.

It is a huge relief to have the weight of the legal battle finally over with especially since we are about to make a move back to Alberta. Now I can concentrate my efforts on finding a place to live and suitable employment. It is the latter part of 2000 by the time we find a home in a small beach town on the shores of Lac St. Anne about 60 kilometers West of Edmonton appropriately named Alberta Beach. It's a beautiful little home close to the water and close to the city. We settle in. Andree finds a job cooking, and I find a job doing some maintenance work, but again the pay is minimal.

As much as we love where we live and would like to stay, seasonal and minimum wage work is all we find, and once more, we move. This time we move to Edmonton. Andree finds work with a cleaning company and I discover that there is a high demand for security guards so I jump in for the training that will guarantee me steady employment. At the beginning, I get mostly night shifts at locations nobody wants requiring a lot of walking in all kinds of weather conditions at construction and utility sites. Then, after I've been there for a while, I hit it lucky and land a position at Canada Place in downtown Edmonton.

At first, I am what they call roaming security, which means I check all the floors in the building, but within a month or so a position at the Conference Center opens up and since I am bilingual in both French and English, I am offered the position. It is a cushy, easy day job to book rooms for dignitaries that come to the city for various conferences as well as looking after setting up the international videoconferences.

I have a good job and I am making a fairly good wage but by 2003 I am so bored that I contemplate setting off all the alarms or jumping out the top-floor window. My co-worker seems to thrive on the same repeating routines but I feel like I'm spinning my wheels and I shudder at continuing with this job. I hand in my resignation.

Andree and I are fed up with city life and feel we both need more meaning and purpose to our lives. We decide to make the trek across the mountains back to BC. This time it will be better. Things will work out. We are sure of it. It has to.

Once in BC, we spend a few days investigating the North Okanagan and fall in love with a beautiful little town of about 5,000 called Armstrong. It has lots of mature trees, overlooking the Spallumcheen Valley and surrounded by dairy and farmland. We settle in Armstrong. The town has a country feel, which we love, and it turns out to be a wonderful place to live. I go back to work as a security guard until I can find work that has more meaning and purpose and will feed the constant hunger of my spirit I've felt for 46 years.

Having found self-expression, depth and the freedom to be in my relationship with Andree, I hungered to find a way to expand this meaning and depth to include my work and all other areas of my life. I still had a nagging emptiness and hunger chewing at my gut all the time.

My previous work as a therapist had silenced that hunger. It allowed me to connect with life and people at a much deeper level than through everyday interactions and it gifted me with meaning, purpose, and a sense of being One with.

The need to be One with, where did that really begin I wonder? Did my need to experience *Oneness* begin with my mother? Maybe even in the womb? Did she ever search for the same thing? Has she ever found it or even glimpsed it? Is there a chance we will ever experience it together?

Questions with no answers.

Dear One:

Truth; is this what leads to Oneness? Truth; is it better to hide it or to speak it, to feel it or to deny it, to live it or to avoid it?

I read a passage by Mark Nepo in "The Book of Awakening," and these words taken from his writing of Feb. 21st called, "Cleaning out the Wound" stay with me.

"..somehow, telling the truth as I know it makes me feel like a bad person-as if I'm making my pain up, as if I'm hurting others by saying bad things about them."

I have felt that a lot.

Now I know.

By speaking my truth I will touch another's truth and it is from this place that the two of us can meet as One.

Need I say more?

Lou

Chapter 44

About Mom

We build from the roots, branch out into who we are and reach towards the light.

Mom, the fourth of six children, lived through her own abandonment experience when her mom, my grandmother, Victoria (Rheaume) Gour, disappeared for seven years to what the doctors described as a semi-comatose state.

She was unresponsive, yet awake, not able to do anything for herself. She no longer recognized her husband and her children and it makes me wonder if without her mom, my mom ever sat at her bedroom window to gaze at the night sky? Did she also search for a sense of connection with something bigger than herself, a connection with a love she couldn't quite reach or wrap her heart around in her world?

When I look back at what it was like for grandma, I suspect the depression preceding her mysterious illness had a lot to do with sheer exhaustion.

From Paincourt, Ontario, she was seventeen years old when she married grandpa and only twenty years old when they moved to Alberta to claim a homestead and open some farmland. By the time she was twenty-seven they had six children and like everyone else who made their way out West to claim a new life for themselves, they struggled to make a living. It was a huge adjustment for grandma. A far cry from the comfortable lifestyle she lived before Grandpa came into her life. A husband, six children ranging from three to twelve years of age, meals to prepare, huge gardens, cows, chickens, horses and pigs to look after and the fast approaching Great Depression of the '30s, all contributed to her breakdown, I'm sure.

My grandfather was devastated but he didn't give up hope and against the doctor's advice to place my grandmother in a hospital or institution, he chose instead to bring her home where she could be surrounded by the people who loved her. His hope was that with the help of his two brothers, who lived only a short distance away and the help of the children, they would be able to look after her and eventually nurse her back to health. Little did he know then that it would take seven years and the birth of another child (as advised by her doctor as the only other possibility that would snap her out of the comatose state), before she could once more become part of their world.

As I think about that now, I can't imagine what it was like for my mom, who from the age of five to twelve lived with a totally unresponsive mother. Instead of having a mother to look after her, she, along with her siblings, were the ones who looked after their mother. They fed her, washed her, brushed her hair, clipped her nails, read to her, and anything else that was required for her care and well-being.

What was going on for my mom as a five-year-old, an eight-year old, or an eleven-year old? Did she have to shut down her emotions? Was this the beginning of her having to pretend everything was all right? Was this where she started to learn to skillfully manoeuvre a pattern of denial and of stuffing her emotions in order to help her survive? Was this the beginning of a shame she buried somewhere deep inside and a continuous fear of what others would say, think, or whisper to each other about her and her family behind her back? Is it why she feared being idle and sitting still, or why she was always so vigilant for signs of depression or mental illness? Did those formative years follow her throughout her life and become a huge part of her? These are the things I will never know for sure.

Mom had a quiet demeanor accented by a non-projecting voice she couldn't make louder no matter how hard she tried to be heard. She was a very determined person with high standards, and she loved learning. She attended a one-room country school and had the same teacher for all eight grades. She wished she could have kept going to school, but by the time she was fifteen, she was already an accomplished cook, baker, housekeeper and child caretaker both in her family home and working with other families. By the age of seventeen, she had married my dad. Much later, when Mom was in her late forties and Dad was in his fifties, after us kids were off on our own, they sold the farm and moved to the Okanagan to escape the harsh Alberta winters.

It didn't take long for their home to become a hub of activity for friends they cherished and loved to entertain. It was as if Mom and Dad's place had a revolving door and everyone that walked through it was more than welcome, but along with the constant entertaining, there also came more drinking.

When I was young, I often felt like an interruption in my mom's life. She was always busy doing, and there was never much time for being. A fear of judgment, perhaps also a residue of her childhood experiences, had set up residence in her back pocket and shadowed her throughout her life.

I learned early on that my needs needed to fit somewhere between her tending to the floor that needed to be polished, the smear on the window that needed to be wiped, the supper that had to be prepared, the dusting, the ironing, or the pot on the stove that was threatening to boil over and was in need of immediate attention. Sometimes I followed her around waiting for those moments when I could catch her in between tasks; other times I went off on my own and I did what, I suspect, she might have also done when she was little which was to pretend or deny that I needed anything at all.

For Mom, like many others of her generation to say, "I love you," was practically unheard of. Her ways of conveying, "I love you," were through a fresh-baked chocolate or lemon meringue pie, polished shoes, a pile of freshly washed and ironed clothes, or a pot of homemade chicken soup to get me through my cold.

As I searched to reach a place of *Oneness* within myself and the world I lived in, I left no stone unturned. It was inevitable that a deeper awareness of things I lived surrounding my mom would come up for me and in May of 1990, I made the following entry in my journal.

May 14, 90

Mom, I don't want to be like you. I don't want to live outside myself the way you have. I want to live from who I am inside. I want to be the real me. For you, what others think and say is important. For me, who I am and how I feel is important. At home, we had to look good, we had to impress and above all, no matter what happened or how we felt inside, we had to keep our head up high, smile, and pretend everything was fine.

You would not, or could not, allow yourself to experience, feel, or be real. I always felt there was something wrong with me because I felt things. I cried, I hurt, I loved, I laughed, I suffered, and I had hopes and dreams, but like a squirrel who hides everything out of necessity, I too hid it all. I hid it from you and the rest of the world.

Now I have to teach myself that there is nothing wrong in allowing others to see what I feel. I have to teach myself that I don't always have to show the world that I am brave and strong and can do it all on my own.

As a little girl, my backpack filled with shame and guilt weighed me down because there were times when the "attention" I was getting from my teacher made me feel good inside. But any good feelings were quickly replaced with yet another round of shame and guilt, and my backpack dug even deeper into my shoulders. I had to find a way not to crumble under the weight. I had to find a way to survive, so after a while I learned to do like you when you were sad, or hurt, or in pain. I blocked things out. I pushed them back. I pretended and I denied.

It was Kevin's death that stopped me. It became a choice of die myself or look at all the hidden, blocked, pushed away pain. I couldn't believe my ears when you told me, "Be strong. Be brave. Don't cry." When I watched you reach for a drink to hide your tears, that's when your way of coping hit me the hardest. Rather than do that, I preferred to go through the pain of Kevin's death and any other pain I had not yet faced and should have.

I love you, Mom, and I know that in your own way you love me, too, and you always have but it saddens me that we have never been able to tell each other this. I can only hope that one day we will be able to say the words we both long to hear.

I am reminded of when Mom tried to make light of things that were happening by telling me there was nothing wrong or by pretending she wasn't hurt by things Dad said. "Everything's fine," The unspoken, "Ignore what you see and hear."

I can hear my child's voice now: It's not fine, damn it! I'm not crazy. I'm not imagining all this; it's there. What I see and what I hear is real. It scares me and I feel alone with my fear. I don't understand why all this is happening, or if it's happening because of me, but you tell me there is absolutely nothing wrong and I wonder what I'm supposed to do with what I see, with what I hear, with the way my stomach feels sick, with the fear running through me? "Go to bed and go to sleep," you tell me. So I crawl far under the blankets, put the pillow over my head so I won't hear the things I know I hear but I'm told I'm imagining, and I find myself wishing tonight would disappear and tomorrow would appear.

Today, even if I am no longer a child, when I am around someone who has had too much to drink, I still freak out. The color drains from my face like water going down the drain, and I either run or freeze in my tracks while inside the feelings are like a tsunami rushing to shore.

I feel fear, sometimes terror. I feel trapped. I feel I'm in danger. I feel powerless. I feel insecure. I feel I have no control. I feel resentful and angry. I feel like a child. I feel my freedom has been taken away. I feel frozen in my fear and I feel sick to my stomach.

The ability to let go of and accept what is, is far from easy for most of us, but I come to realize that my ability to flow with changes, no matter what the changes are, affects how I journey through life transitions and difficult times. Flowing with change is something that challenges Mom. When my father dies in 2002, it creates a very difficult adjustment for Mom to live through and for the next four or five years, little by little, her health starts to deteriorate as she tries to come to terms with the death of the man who was her partner for sixty-three years.

Complicating that adjustment, she has to depend on and accept more and more help from others. A year after Dad dies, Mom has to make a move into an assisted living home, which is also a difficult transition. Then, from August of 2004 to August of 2006, Mom comes to live with Andree and me.

It is a time filled with moments of joy, celebration and pride mixed with moments of frustration, concern, worry and pain and sometimes sheer despair, but every day while she is in our care I am grateful for the time I spend with her.

The happy moments when we laugh and share some good times become fewer and the difficult ones increase and are more of a challenge for us to handle. It is sad to watch my mom's life fall apart around her. I see a side of her that is beautiful and a part of her that is screaming to be let out. There are times when there is an angered, resentful, stubborn woman who lives inside her body.

Other times I see a side of her I can't help but love—times when I push her on the wooden swing hanging beneath the big weeping willow in our front yard, and she hangs on for dear life fearful of losing her balance, yet clearly loving the feeling of freedom it gives her, or times when she comes alive as she pitches in and helps Andree roll out the pie dough or drop the cookies on the cookie sheet. There are the times she comes with me to feed a carrot to the horses and she shares memories of when she had her own horse. Then there are the many times she gets a great big grin on her face when she suggests we go for a caramel sundae. "My treat," she says with excitement in her voice as all three of us jump in the car and head out to Dairy Queen where she enjoys her ice cream to the very last drop.

Then there are the harder times when it isn't always easy for her, or for us. Her Parkinson's robs her of her last vestiges of privacy. Medication adjustments, increased loss of balance leading to more falls demands all of our attention. Her anger, bitterness, resentment and fear grows as her independence decreases. It breaks me apart.

When Mom came to live with us, I let go of the night work doing security jobs and I took a job at the Coop gas station only a few blocks from home. It is a very busy place but it gives me full time employment and daytime work. Things go well and I don't mind the work, but physically I am suffering. I require major surgery to remove, tuck, sew and repair parts of my female anatomy, and as a result standing on my feet for eight hours a day is no longer an option.

I jump on the computer to investigate the feasibility of returning to counselling as a career. After much homework, legwork and a colossal amount of forms and paper work, I receive grants to pay for my schooling and I'm accepted into an intense one-year counselling program in Kelowna.

Taking the program requires that I travel one hour to school every morning and one hour back home to Armstrong every night, but it is the only thing that makes sense to do. I've been away from this work I love for far too long. Andree looks after Mom and everything at home during the day, and I take over Mom's care when I get back home from school. In the evening, once Mom is bathed and settled, I begin my studies. For a year, that's how we carry on.

Dear One:

Here it is. Here's my truth of the moment. I'm caught between a piece of heaven and a piece of hell. I have in some way, at some level, what I've always wanted. My situation is as close to perfect as it can get.

The year is 2004 and I live in a nice big home on the outskirts of a beautiful little town called Armstrong in a lush mountain valley in the North Okanagan of BC. There are friendly neighbors on three sides but we don't actually see each other. It's very private.

The patio doors off the kitchen open to a large deck that faces farmland that's being used as a pasture for horses and I often go feed them an apple or a carrot pretending they're my own. In the morning or in the evening after the sun has gone down, the deer come, graze with the horses, and give us the best of both worlds in our own backyard.

Another near perfect world; or at least the perfect set-up for a perfect world – a world of possibilities; for three people to have the opportunity to live in truth and to live the essence of who they are. Or at least that's what I hoped for.

Dreams and visions are sometimes hard to hold on to in the face of reality, the unforeseen or the unexpected. Right now, I'm tired. Exhausted. The hope that propelled me forward is fraught with challenges. Some I fully expected while others have crept out of nowhere and slapped me upside the head like I'd been hit with a 2X4.

Right now, I live a duality; a piece of heaven and a piece of hell which sit next to each other in our home, and within my heart and soul.

Voicing truth, living authenticity, making connection and experiencing Oneness, is there a way to actually live it with those who resist having it as part of their life?

Lou

Chapter 45

A Piece of the Journey

The essence of truth is love, expansion and expression and Oneness is the result.

I need to mother the mother in some ways I feel I never had. It should be as simple as tying my shoes or as simple as saying, "I love you," but it isn't. Words, at least true ones, or meaningful ones, are as rare as pearls in oysters at the bottom of the sea.

I get sucked into her world as if trapped in the wake of a boat where she's at the helm. If I'm not being washed over with negativity, it's unexpected remarks. They drain my energy. They force me further and further under the water keeping me from breaking the surface for air.

I'm drowning in a pool of guilt, only I can't figure out if it's mine or hers. Or does it come from the frustrations of the present day. Nothing is ever simple anymore. Things have become too hard, too long, too complicated, too loud, too high, too dark, too fast, too negative, too something, and I find myself questioning.

What is real? Mom's truth continues to be something that hides backstage.

"Did you like your piece of pie Mom?"

"It was good, but it was way too sweet."

"Did you have fun at the park today Mom?"

"Yes, but it was too hot."

"Isn't it a nice day today, Mom?"

"Yes, but it's supposed to rain tomorrow."

"Do you want to go to town, Mom?"

"No, but I suppose I have to follow."

She has a voice but rarely is it an accurate reflection of what she feels inside. I'm always trying to peer around the corner, look beyond, dig deeper, to try and find the real meaning behind the words she speaks. It's a dance we've had since forever. Is she tired, is she depressed, does she miss my father, is she angry with herself, me, life? It's like a brainteaser puzzle I can't decipher. But she's my mom. I don't want to feel frustrated. I want to care for her, pull her close and love her. Oh, if it were that simple.

The heavy hollow feeling in my chest conjures an image from long ago. She stands in the kitchen of the old farmhouse in the Peace Country, where unlike here the sky goes on forever like a giant dome over Alberta's prairie land. She feeds my dad's long johns, my assorted color T-shirts and her cotton dresses between the rollers of the old wringer washing machine.

I stand on my tippy-toes on a chair beside her. I watch mesmerized. The sight and sound of the air and the water that squishes out of the clothes fascinates me. When they come out the other side, every piece is flattened like road-kill. They fall in a heap at the bottom of a big galvanized tub. Lifeless. Still. Waiting.

It reminds me of how my stomach feels when I hold my breath, wait and wonder what is going to happen next.

But as I look now, I see Mom's lips curl slightly upwards and her dark brown eyes fill with light. I recognize this look. It speaks of what I've come to know as pride, and it lets me know she's satisfied with a job well done. This sense of pride she exudes in her work seeps under my skin like an underground tributary. I emulate her but I do not want to be like her. Perhaps this is where it all began, this insatiable need to seek *Oneness* and voice.

It's this search for *Oneness* that propels me forward in the need to care for my mom. Part of me sees this as an opportunity to right wrongs, live truths and to understand the unfinished puzzle. Maybe that's where things started going wrong a long time ago; in my assuming I could make things better for her, for us; or maybe it's where things begin to go right.

Maybe in some kind of selfish way I want her to find her voice thinking it will help me find mine. Maybe hiding in the back of my mind, I think I can help her touch her truth. And in some kind of naive way, I think maybe I can do that with her or maybe even do it for her. It takes me a long time to learn that I can't take people where they aren't willing to go.

But in this moment, in the middle of taking care of my mom and dealing with her stubborn and contrary ways, my frustration mounts and I have a hard time to connect with what I've learned. Instead, I wonder how to keep the hungry vicious wolves of unexpressed anger and resentment away.

I bring shame upon myself for having to scrape the bottom of the barrel to touch my compassionate side right now. The loving caring person I know I am has a hard time rising to the surface when caught in a cross fire of opposites.

And I wonder, *"How will I ever untangle myself from this intrinsic web of love, shame and fear?"*

My inside voice scolds, *"Don't be so impatient, so frustrated, so mad."*

My thoughts don't reflect my love for her. They make my stomach feel like all my loving compassionate parts are getting squished out of me like when I watched the water squish out of the clothes going through that old wringer washing machine. I need to be the grownup here.

I steal another glance at her as I leave the room. Her face is drawn, her skin pasty, transparent like onion skin paper, and her lips, slight, almost disappear without the lipstick she usually wears. Her wavy black hair is adorned with just enough grey streaks to give her an air of distinction as an elderly woman in her mid-eighties. She's sitting in her rocking chair where I've set her up with her morning coffee, a glass of water, her magazine, a supply of tissues, her blanket and the remote control for her TV.

She has a curvature of the spine and a hip that gives her grief and results in her sitting or walking with a slight tilt to the right. She is a tiny woman but her grip is surprisingly strong. It's a strength she's gathered over the many hard years of work on the farm. My eyes well with tears at the sight of her diminutive frame which appears smaller every time I turn around. And my heart goes out to her when I see how frustrated she gets with a mind that often plays "catch me if you can."

I wonder what life has brought to her that she's never shared and where the time to make amends or create changes has gone. She is set in her ways, weighed down by resentment, anger, and the many things that remain unresolved. I wonder if it's too late, or even fair of me to poke around in a morass of lifetimes gone by? Does she, or has she ever felt a desire to have things different for herself or am I the one who's wanted that? Am I perhaps the only one who feels she can benefit if she deals with, let's go of, or makes peace with, aspects of herself and experiences she's had?

Whether it was needed or not needed, she has always been a woman who has busied herself. The constant pressure to "do" has followed her to the place where she is now—a place where she struggles to hold on to independence, a place where she often gets frustrated and angry because there is much she can no longer do for herself, and having to ask for help is akin to having to cut off her own arm.

I have no trouble with that. I can step into her shoes and understand. But what I can't understand or do anything about is that no matter how much I want to, I can't help her accept what is or to open her arms and let me in.

It's a big jump across the abyss. It is hard for her to realize she used to look after me and now I need to be the one to look after her. This gradual decline she can see happening is complex and scary. It's like having to swim across the English Channel and not having a clue how to swim.

She's found ways to ask for help without really asking. When she says, "I would have to put my shoes on." It means, "I need help to get them on." When she says, "I would need to take a bath." It means, "I can't do that by myself but it sure would feel good to have one." She is a proud woman who has always had to forge her own way. To ask for help is hard; to accept help is even harder.

It breaks my heart to see all the other little changes that are happening with her. Little things like the need to carry a Kleenex in her hand at all times. The need to constantly wipe the coffee drips on the side of her cup. The almost compulsive trips back and forth to the bathroom every few minutes and how she has a need to watch the clock like a time keeper whose life depends on it—all these things become an obsession and the focus of her day. Some days I can make light of these quirks and accept that they become part of my day too, other days I feel cheated and deprived of spontaneity and want to rip every damn clock off the wall.

I want to take the guilt that sits inside me and sweep it into a heap the way I do when I sweep the dust bunnies and breadcrumbs off the kitchen floor. Guilt is insidious. It sneaks into little crevices and slinks around like black coal dust that makes it hard for me to breathe, and has a way of eating away at the good stuff.

I question what I got myself into when I brought us all here to live together and what it is I feel as the demands of her care increase and her situation becomes more and more unpredictable. There are days when my partner and I look at each other and wonder how on earth we'll survive.

Yes, I have chosen to be here. It was what my heart told me to do. It was the right thing. I have no doubt about that.

Mom is not well lately. She is down to ninety-two pounds. When she walks around in the house, unless she hits a squeaky floor board, she's like a ghost who walks on air. Some days we start thinking she won't see Christmas she's so tiny and so frail. Other days she surprises us and bounces back with a glimpse of the 'piss and vinegar' her body once had. She never rebounds as high.

There's not much left for her to live for and some nights I find myself asking Dad, who's already gone to the other side to come for her. Then I feel shitty, like I'm trying to play some kind of God with the thoughts that sneak into my mind.

Often I ask myself just what I am I supposed to do with this guilt? Am I supposed to tuck it into my back pocket and hope to forget? I scold myself for even thinking my life is on hold when her life is rolling ever closer to an end.

But all of that doesn't take away the fact that it's difficult to live my own life when it's hanging in the rafters, not knowing if Mom will still be there tomorrow, the day after, next week, next month or next year. I keep on with a life that can't be attached to a plan. So I wait.

I wait to see what I can commit to and what I can't. I wait to see how much I will be needed and when. I wait and I wait and I wait - not for her to die, but to know what I should do, when, where, and how because it depends on her condition; today could be entirely different from tomorrow and I have to be ready to adjust my life to what today brings.

One minute, I'm okay. I don't want it any other way. The next minute I realize how our lives are completely consumed by hers, I am exhausted and I drag my belly on the ground.

I can't plan, think ahead, or discuss where I will go or what will happen. All I can do is wait and see, because there are always unknowns. But the one thing I do know is that my life will change drastically when she is gone, and it's painful to think about what that will be like and how much I will miss her when that happens. It makes me realize that it's not so much what I have to do for her that weighs me down, it's the things I can't do, like helping her find her voice and her words, and helping her live the *Oneness* she so much deserves.

I fall into bed exhausted and drift off to sleep. In the wee hours of the morning images dance across the screen of my mind. There's an image of my mom superimposed on the child fading in and out, to an image of a child superimposed on the mother. I toss and turn until I decide to get up and scribble my unspoken words in my journal.

I Feel:

~love for the woman who gave me life
~guilt about feeling trapped, about wanting it to be over for her
~guilt about writing and talking about her to others
~unsure how to proceed with her care without taking her dignity and hurting her pride
~judged by others on the care we provide
~scared because I can't hear the whispers of my heart anymore
~sad, to witness my mom so unhappy in her life
~frustrated with the complexities of it all
~fear of what's to come and how it will turn out
~ trapped in a role reversal
~tired of the tension, the lack of sleep, the unknown
~inadequate to make my love penetrate, touch and heal

I fight with the love I feel for Mom mixed with thoughts that I wish she would die. Her world has been stripped of color. She seems to have nothing to do, say, or live for. I would hope she is in the best place – where simply being is okay, but she doesn't seem to live it that way at all.

I feel her fear as she gets closer and closer to the chasm between two worlds and the mystery and uncertainty that surrounds it all and of not knowing when it will happen or how. It must be awful to sit through the day and wait because there's nothing to do but wait for lunch, or dinner, or bedtime, or for the end to come.

I'm drained, absolutely drained and so is my partner. I hear her say, "I have to find a way to cope. I have to find some coping skills." I feel I should have something to offer, something I could suggest or say, a line I could throw out for her to grab so she won't drown, but some days I draw a blank. I have nothing to offer. I'm drowning, too.

My partner and I are both exhausted and unless someone has lived or is living this experience, it's impossible to explain the constant fog we find ourselves living in.

Sometimes I look forward to the day when I won't have to be responsible for another person's well-being, when I won't have to explain my every move, forward or backwards, when I won't have to worry about how to fill the silence with empty words about things that don't matter. I crave for meaning, truth, and words that come from the heart and match reality.

Life as I once knew it no longer is. There's a great big hole where the wind blows through what my life once was. It nips away at peace, solitude and sanity. Sometimes I feel guilty for feeling all these things, and sometimes I watch helplessly as even hope slips quietly away.

It's not as if I don't know how to be there for others. I have, after all raised four children of my own, but with a child, you move forward into progress; with an aging parent, you move backwards into decline.

I have to stand straight and tall. Time will alter life as it always does, and I know one day I'll look back and see that the wind wasn't as strong as I thought it was.

By August of 2006, we can no longer look after Mom. The family makes the decision to move her into a nursing home. It is tough to see her go. I shed many tears, some of frustration, anger, guilt, but also of relief, plus a deep sense of having failed, mixed with moments of knowing we have done our best.

Dear One:

I am filled with regret that it couldn't have been more than it was and in some ways relieved that it's over.

How do I reconcile one with the other?

Lou

Chapter 46

Oneness Revealed

A need for connection is also a need for self-expression.

I am saddened to see the kind of life Mom is living now. It's the kind of situation no one wants for their own end.

Yesterday, on my way back home, I stopped in to give her a bath the way I did every night when she was at our home. After her bath, I cleaned her nails, brushed her hair, brushed her teeth, helped her to bed and tucked her in. Her mind was confused ninety percent of the time.

I stopped in to see her again tonight and was hoping things had improved but again she was confused, frustrated, angry and at times, rude. Whatever I said only seemed to make things worse. I can certainly understand how hard it must be to feel like a prisoner of her mind and of her body. It has to be hard to accept to see herself no longer being able to do simple tasks like getting a Kleenex, pouring a drink for herself or going to the bathroom. It's hard to always have to depend on and be at the mercy of others.

A mixed bag of emotions sits in the pit of my stomach when I see her like this. Sometimes I wonder if she suffers, or if it's we who suffer from seeing her. Sometimes I wish she would die in her sleep instead of being where she never wanted to be or in a condition she never wanted to see herself in. Then I hate myself for having such awful thoughts.

I wonder, too, if one shouldn't be able to choose life or death when we get to that point. But then when would one make that decision, and what would be the defining line between staying here and checking out?

Feb. 14/07

Mom. You would not allow life to enter you. To do so also meant to allow your pain. So you shut the doors and shut them so tight, I couldn't open them to see the real you. You locked yourself in, tucked yourself so far back in the darkness that I think even you forgot who you were.

Today I go visit you in the nursing home, and your physical self is also a prisoner now. You can no longer run away to sweep the floor or escape to clean the spot on the window. You probably can no longer even run away in your own mind.

My visits with her are filled with bittersweet moments now. It's upsetting to see some of the changes that are happening for her, but it's also exciting when I am fortunate enough to witness a glimpse of the real her emerging. Often there's a puzzled look on her face as she surprises herself and I see her wonder who that is poking through the façade that has been her saving grace through the years. And I wonder too, who is this woman, who every now and then breaks the surface like a sunburst through a cloud.

I go visit her. I give her a bath. I put her nightgown on. I help her into bed, tuck her in and place her stuffed puppy under her arm. I lean over, kiss her goodnight, and a lump the size of a hardboiled egg sits in the back of my throat. As I stand and start to walk away one of my tears falls on her pillow, mingles with hers and for a minute, I swear my heart stops.

The next day I go see Mom again and she is a mess. Her mind is off in some other world and she is paranoid and angry. In a way, I wish I could stay with her forever, reassure her, make her feel better, and calm her down. But another part of me wants to leave because it doesn't seem to make any difference to her if I am there or not, and all I want to do is to run and run and cry and cry.

All her life she swallowed her words and held back what she had to say, and now she tries so hard to get words out and no words come. She's buried things so deep that her words are out of reach, or they're just not there anymore. Her words have died inside her.

I'm afraid for her. I'm afraid for me.

I don't want my words to die inside of me.

Between my two sisters and me there is someone visiting Mom almost every day. When my brother Richard comes down from Alberta and stays for a few days, he goes every day for as many days as he is here.

Every second or third day or so I am the one to go visit her. I squat on my heels beside her wheel chair. Usually her eyes are closed, and I touch her lightly and call out her name.

"Mom. Hello, Mom, how are you today?"

Every time I see her, the response is different. Sometimes she opens her eyes and it is plain to see she is very pleased to see me. Her eyes light up and she has a huge smile. Other times she looks at me with tears in her eyes, and when I ask, "What's wrong? Why are you crying?" She tells me she is tired, or she wants to get out of there, or she just doesn't know why except that she feels like crying.

I tell her, "It is okay, Mom. You can cry," and I reach for the Kleenex she is unable to reach so I can wipe the tears for her. I rub her back, hold her hand, and ask if she wants to talk about it. Sometimes she does. She tells me about how she doesn't want to live there, or how she doesn't want to be in the wheelchair that she can't get out of, that she wants to quit breathing and not wake up anymore.

I hold her hand tighter hoping that somehow it will help ease her pain, or is it my pain or are they the same? I don't know anymore. My pain, her pain, is there a difference I wonder? Both of us have suffered. Both of us have been through so much and I wonder if our pain is meshed together as One.

It was like that between her and me at times, she not wanting or never able to touch her pain, me living it, feeling it for her. Me playing the catcher, the runner, the holder of what was inside of her that she was unable to get out or never dared to speak about. She feared that if she opened the door she would never be able to close it again and that is the saddest thing of all.

Sept. 1/07

I went to see Mom again tonight. We can't have much of a conversation anymore. When she does talk, I can't hear much of what she's says. Out of what I do hear, about half of it doesn't make sense, so it doesn't leave much I can respond to. She eats well though. Always cleans her plate and eats whatever they give her.

Sept. 16/07

I had a nice visit with Mom this morning. I was with her for three hours. We shared some laughs. I love to see her burst into laughter. I so rarely saw that in her, especially in her later years. In many ways, I enjoy being with her now more than I ever have because she's so much more real. She can't put on a show anymore. Her guard is down and without the pretense; she's so much more authentic than she ever has been. She can't pretend about being or not being pleased or happy or mad, she just is whatever she is. And it's so beautiful.

A shade has been drawn and another has lifted. She is less and less who she tried to be and more and more who she is. I can do things and say things to her I never could have before. I hold her hand, I rub her back, I pamper her, wash her face, brush her hair, fix her nails and put lotion on her. I do what needs to be done like bathroom calls, dressing, undressing, bathing and sometimes I help her eat. I push her in her wheelchair, I tuck her into bed, and I kiss her goodnight. I feel honored that I am allowed to love her now.

Oct. 14/07

I'm writing from Mom's room at the home. I've been here for two hours already. I'll be staying to help her with her lunch. I've got her relaxing in her chair right now. She's tired but this is actually one of her better days.

Jan. 4/08

Mom didn't look all that great yesterday.

Jan.28/08

Mom was sick to her stomach just before I got there. She was slumped over in her chair, eyes shut, hands closed into fists, cold and unresponsive.

I got her a straw for the drink sitting in front of her that she can't reach or hold even if she is thirsty. I wheel her over to her room and put a blanket over her to try to warm her. I get her to drink little sips here and there while I continue to try to get responses from her.

A few times she mutters a word or two, which I can't make out, and then she is quiet again, eyes closed seemingly oblivious to my presence. I pull up a chair close to her and let my eyes drift around the room. A picture of her and Dad taken the day they were married hangs on the wall facing her bed. Next to it is a brown frame with an anniversary poem and a clock that marks the passing of time. Another frame holds a picture of her grandchildren and there's also one of her son and her three daughters.

In the corner, a cabinet holds the things that are precious to her. There are a few pieces of crystal, some fancy delicate china cups, some 25th and 50th anniversary gifts, and other various pieces of memorabilia.

The climbing ivy, the prayer plant and the broad leaf rubber-like plant also helps to make her room look more like home. All of that and a few other things like decorative colors around the big window where she looks out help to bring warmth to the sterile room.

Maybe it helps to have those things there to remind her and comfort her, but sometimes I wonder if maybe it is more for our comfort than for hers. Right then, at the moment when I am holding her hand and looking at her, none of that matters. What matters is that each breath she takes is followed by another and another.

She looks tired, uncomfortable and helpless. I want to hold her in my arms, rock her gently back and forth, and make all her pain go away. Hold her and rock her for all the times her mother, who was in a coma, never could.

I wish I could ease things for her but all I can do is hold her hand and send her all the positive energy I can.

On February 25, 2008, we celebrate Mom's eighty-sixth birthday. In many ways, she is more lost than ever and in some way I feel more connected to her than ever. How sad that we couldn't have shared this before, yet, how wonderful to have found it now.

March 18/08

Mom is not well. She didn't eat and hardly drank all day. She wouldn't even open her eyes. Her blood pressure was excessively high. She told me she would die soon. Maybe she knows.

I feel a lot of guilt and sadness that Andree and I couldn't keep Mom with us. Especially when I see her deteriorate and not have the care I wish we could have given her.

Mom no longer living with us, means we can no longer afford to keep the big house we are living in. We have to find something smaller and more affordable.

It is hard to give up the home and the town we have grown to love but financially we have no choice. The housing market has gone sky high and it is almost impossible to find something we can afford. It takes several months but eventually we find something in Kelowna. Neither one of us is keen on moving there, but it seems to be the only choice and the best choice to make in order to start my counselling practice.

Starting my business is slow at first but through trial and error, I learn what works and what doesn't work. Once I have that going I decide to further my studies once more. I register to do a Bachelor of Science in Psychology. I challenge a few of the courses, pass them and I work hard to complete the rest. While working and studying I continue to visit Mom at the nursing home and on the 20th of August, 2008, at the age of fifty six, I complete my studies and attain my degree.

I have reached a place I have been inching towards for years I am back to doing the kind of work that resonates with who I am and that allows me to live the gifts I have. I am in the right place, doing what is right for me.

On another level, the *Oneness* I intellectually learned about and have emotionally and spiritually craved presents itself to me in my relationship with my partner, with Emily, with my family, with nature, and in my relationship with others, but the most precious and most rewarding experience of *Oneness* comes from the relationship I experience with my mom.

Dear One:

There are things I want to say. It's hard to find the words, but I know it has to do with the magic held within an open heart.

It's when people's hearts are open that real life takes place. That's why I loved the kind of work I did at an agency whose focus was to be there for the people, and that's why I love the work I do now as a counsellor.

It's also why I love doing retreats, journal writing groups and other types of workshops. Those are places and times where people touch the truth of who they are – where they touch the sacred within themselves—this is the place that I always crave to live from.

I'm grateful that my visits with Mom are helping me reach a much deeper understanding of this place of truth and connection that can be summarized by one word. To me, "Oneness" says it all.

Lou

Chapter 47

More Connections

Sometimes it takes us forever to learn something simple. We have to learn it in a hundred different ways before we can say, ah ha! Now I get it!

My visits with Mom in the past few days make me think even more about *Oneness* and what it means.

I put Mom to bed and tell her, "Goodnight, sleep tight, don't let the bedbugs bite," and she responds with, "And if they do, take your shoe and hit them until they're black and blue." It's what used to happen when I was a child, only it used to be me going to bed and her leaving the room. That's a moment of connection.

Then there's the time when she and I were alone at the house, and she came to me almost foaming at the mouth with anger and contempt as she confronted me about Andree and I living together. At that time Andree and I had been together for eight or nine years, the last two of which all three of us lived under the same roof. Her face is red and her words come out like venom, "I know what you're doing. I know what's going on with you and Andree. I'm not stupid. I know what's happening. You're a lesbian!" This is a moment of truth being spoken.

There are the days when I visit her at the home and we share precious time together when I put her nail polish on, curl her hair, or freshen up her face with a warm face cloth and put her lipstick on. Looking good is so important for her, and she says, "That feels so much better." That is love and connection in action.

There are times when I sit close to her, my arm leaning on the tray attached to her wheelchair, and she gently passes her hand over the hair on my arm and says, "You have lots of fur on your arms," and we both laugh. Or she looks at someone coming down the hallway and turns to me and voices the thoughts going through her head, "She's dressed funny." Instead of thinking one thing and saying another, the words she speaks match the thoughts. They are genuine and real - more real than they have ever been and I love it. Those are moments of authenticity.

And then there is the day I wheel her over to the other wing of the building. When I get there, the residents are having a sing-a-long. The director of activities is playing a DVD of hit songs from the era when the residents were young.

The magic blows me away. Some of the people singing can't carry a conversation on a good day. Here they are singing every word, in time for every beat. Everyone's face is lit up with smiles and a surge of clapping and hoorays follow at the end of each song. *Oh Susanna. She'll Be Coming Around the Mountain, Goodnight Irene.*

I look at Mom and her eyes are closed but her lips are moving. She is trying to join in. I wheel her closer and sit down beside her. When the next song starts, I sing out loud and she pipes in with the words for the verses coming to her as if they have been waiting all this time to be set free. I look at one of the staff members, "It's bloody amazing!"

She responds, "It's in here," as she lifts a hand to her heart.

For the first time in my life, Mom and I sing together. It's not such a big deal for mother and daughter to do that, but for us, it is unheard of. It is an intimate moment I hold close to my heart. In that moment we connect at a level that goes beyond pretending, fears, hurts, or any misunderstandings that might have existed between us. It is authenticity at its best.

Those moments are like gold nuggets. Moments where she is okay to be who she is. Moments I crave and need – the person she was always meant to be. The real her. The person I always looked for but could never find.

Now there is only being present and being real. And being real in that moment is an older woman, weathered by ups and downs of life, sitting in her wheelchair, singing a song to which she always knew the words but could never allow herself to sing out loud.

I feel totally blessed to sit beside her and to witness her finally singing her song. This is a moment of *Oneness* lived.

Dear One:

I feel a need to share with you the things I've learned from my parents.

From my father I learned to always be willing to help and to be there for others in whatever way I could. I learned the dedication one can have to their work, but also the importance of rewarding oneself once the work is done and I learned that I can decide for myself what is right for me. From him I also learned how I didn't want to be treated as a woman and I learned how much destruction alcohol can bring.

From my mother I got strength, perseverance and determination and from her, too, I learned how I didn't want to be treated as a woman. Through her denial of feelings and of not living the truth of who she was, I learned that I needed and wanted different for myself. I learned how important it is to have a voice, how easy it is to lose it, and how difficult it is to find it once it has been lost.

From both of them, by way of example, I learned to work hard and to do things well. Through them, due to them, in spite of, and because of them, I am who I am today. I needed who they were and who they weren't in order to become who I was meant to be.

Lou

Chapter 48

Reflections – My Mother or Yours

I will step out of the way and let my voice be heard.

I looked at Mom, now 87 years old. There didn't seem to be much left of her. As I looked at her, I wondered if I would also end up living in a home and needing constant care like her.

We all hope we won't have to end our lives unable to look after ourselves in our later years. We all want to somehow come to the end of this life in a graceful manner, to die peacefully in our sleep before our body deteriorates or our mind short circuits.

I know it's what Mom hoped for - to end her life in a different way. I hoped to help her do that by taking her in to live with us, but I couldn't carry it through to the end and I fear for her care now with everything that is happening at the home. There are changes in ownership, in staffing, in rules and regulations. There are cutbacks and people in higher places look at running a "business" more so than a "care facility." It's sad to see how things are often about the dollar rather than the people's well-being. I wish Mom wasn't there to experience any of this. I wish I could protect her from these changes, which are bound to drastically affect her care.

And affect her care it does.

The changes happening in the home where Mom lives prompts me to use my voice sending a letter to the people responsible. The letter reads:

I found Mom slumped over in the dining room in her tilted back chair with her legs dangling in midair. There was a white chalky trail that started from her eyes to the bottom of her cheeks where tears had run down her face. When I knelt down beside her, took her hand in mine and asked her how she was doing, her voice became agitated. She started to shake.

I am enraged her needs have been ignored.

She may not have modelled for me how to speak my words but I can speak for her now. Her words deserve to be heard - bend down, put your ear next to her and take the time to listen. And if you take the time to do this you might realize that there is an adult stuck inside what now functions as a child's body. (Needing our care, respect and attention.)

Why does my head keep spinning today, twenty-four hours after I've been to visit my mom? My head keeps spinning because when I took mom to her room, she was increasingly agitated and frustrated. When I finally managed to calm her down enough to quit shaking and to speak to me, she said she needed to go to the bathroom.

It took me half a minute to get her there. Not quick enough, she could no longer hold on, and as I transferred her from her wheel chair to the toilet, she urinated on the floor. And as I sat her on the toilet she had to go even more. This means she needed to go for a long time.

My mom is not incontinent. She has very good bladder control. Her problem is not holding on, but that she cannot get to the bathroom on her own. And if no one takes the time to bend down and ask her, she cannot make herself heard.

As my mom sat on the toilet and I washed her tear stained face, she said to me, "I have never been so ashamed in my life." And my head is spinning because I can still hear her words, and I can still see my prim and proper mother who always took pride in her appearance sitting on the toilet with mismatched dirty clothes. I've never seen her look so sad. My head is spinning because I can hear her and be there for her now in a way she wasn't able to be there for me. Yet I can't stop you, you meaning all her caregivers from front line to management to board and owners, from ignoring her, from the dangers and harm of understaffing.

My head is spinning because I can see the difference between tears of sensitivity to light and tears of frustration, anger and indignation.

For the most part, there are good staff working in Mom's home, and some of them are absolute models of what caring and compassion should be. There are two who deliver such amazing care and every staff member should be trained by them. When those two, or people like them, are on shift, the whole establishment runs smoothly. Not only are the residents happy, smiling and content, but so are the family members who visit them.

People who work in a home for the elderly shouldn't even be hired unless they are there to do what they love. Love late, love early, love at the end of life is better than not at all. Maybe we should consider the dignity we can offer our aging parents by being *One* with them. You might also want to keep in mind that all of us are next in line.

Dear One:

It's in the process of putting words on the page that movement happens within me and movement is what helps to take things a step further and helps to create change.

Thank you for helping me find my voice and for helping me speak the words my mom cannot speak.

It has been a gift, a reverse healing of sorts, to be given the opportunity to be a voice for both of us.

Lou

Chapter 49

Coming Full Circle

Relationships are the muscles of my heart.

Mom was not feeling well for a few days, and on August 15th she took a turn for the worse.

I'm sitting at Mom's bedside. I hope someone from above comes to get her. It's not right for people to have such a rough time when they're approaching their time to leave this world.

She is experiencing night tremors. Maybe these were happening before but we didn't know because we've never actually spent the night at her bedside. Her body cramps up, her hands make fists, her arms and legs get drawn into herself, her face tightens and her whole body gets tied in a knot like a wrung out dishcloth.

She doesn't say anything or make any sounds, but I imagine she must be in terrible pain when her body goes into these spasms. When they're happening, they totally consume her.

My brother is here from Alberta; my two sisters are here, too. We've decided one of us will stay with her all the time now. I'm taking the first shift tonight.

Sunday Aug. 16/09 - 8:15 am

The sun is out. Mom made it through the night. It was wicked. Her body was continually going into spasms. She shook so bad that the whole bed rattled even with me sitting on it. Every part of her gets drawn tight like strings on a banjo. It's awful to see and it breaks my heart not to be able to make it stop.

She's settled and resting now after an Ativan and a Tylenol suppository have been administered. Her breathing is calm and her body looser, more relaxed. I spent the night sitting in a chair by her side, and when her body went into spasms, almost every half hour, I leaned over and held her close making sure her fingers and arms didn't dig into her frail, fragile body.

When the spasms subsided, I rubbed her muscles to try to relax them and rolled her into a different position so she would be more comfortable. In the moments in between her seizures, even though I'm not a religious person, I prayed for those who have gone before her, my dad, my son Kevin and my nephew Mike to come for her. It is gut-wrenching to see her go through this, and as I watched over her, I couldn't help but think that in her approaching death, like in her life, she seemed to be holding on and unable to let go.

1:40 pm

Mom is still not doing well. She is not awake much. It's better if she doesn't get better. I think it's best if she goes.

4:15 pm

I slept for one and a half hours. My first sleep since Friday night.

My sisters, my brother and I discuss what is happening with Mom, then my sister Danielle, who is the one designated to make decisions on Mom's behalf, speaks with the doctor. He agrees to our request, to only do what is necessary to keep Mom comfortable. This is in line with Mom's wishes.

A butterfly is put into Mom's arm to dispense morphine when needed to alleviate her suffering. It will give her some relief and when the time is right, it will allow her to let go more peacefully. A good portion of her life has been about hanging on. She's struggled long enough. It's time for her to finally let go.

6:30 pm

Mom is resting peacefully. She doesn't struggle anymore. They are supposed to give her more morphine at seven pm so she will continue to rest peacefully. The bed looks too big for her tiny body. There's not much of her left. We don't know how much longer she will be here. It depends on the strength of her heart. My brother, my sisters and I will stay with her tonight.

Monday Aug. 17/09 – 7:27 am

Mom just took her last breath. She is gone.

RIP: Yvonne Labrecque – February 25th, 1922 - August 17th, 2009.

When my brother and my two sisters are finished saying goodbye and leave to take care of other matters, I stay in the room with Mom for close to an hour. I sit in the bed with my back against the headboard and I hold her in my arms, stroke her hair, rock her, sing to her and love her into her next life.

Song:

We are One, we are One
I am you, you are me
And we are One
And in this unity
We do live in harmony
For peace has come
And we are *One*

Sept. 8/09

I need to find my center. I asked Spirit to take my mom. Now, for selfish reasons, I would like to ask that she be given back to me. I miss seeing her. I miss feeling her physical presence, and I miss feeling that maybe my presence mattered, perhaps even made a difference in her life in her last few years.

I miss washing her face with a warm face cloth, feeding her, tucking her into bed and kissing her goodnight. I miss watering her plants, washing her clothes, pushing her in her wheelchair and bringing her outside to smell the flowers. I miss her sometimes-witty remarks and her iron grip on my arms when I helped her out of her wheelchair and put her to bed. I miss drying and styling her hair and seeing the smile on her face when I brought her a root beer. I miss her bony, shaky hands reaching up to me to try to fasten the last few buttons on my shirt and I miss bringing her chocolate rose buds and chocolate mints.

I miss the things she could not give like - touches, "I love you"', protection, undivided attention and time. And I miss all the ways she made up for it with piles of freshly washed and ironed clothes, homemade chocolate and lemon meringue pies or her constant worry about me. I miss our arm wrestling days of eons past and the times we shared laughs. I even miss the closed-off surface person she used to be and the more genuine open person she became as her coping skill of pretending slowly faded away.

I know there are many times when I swore I would not make the same mistakes she did, that I would make different choices and walk my own path and I did, and I'm proud of that. But as I look back I realize that my own path wasn't necessarily free of mistakes either, and likely my own children are saying they too will learn from my mistakes and walk a different path than I. And I realize that's how it should be with one generation learning from the other in order to create more balanced individuals living full and productive lives.

The thing is, I didn't only learn from her mistakes. I also learned from her strength, determination, stubbornness, will power and resilience, which made her who she was, and is now part of who I am.

From her I learned that when I fall down I can pick myself up and keep going. I learned that where there's a will, there's a way. I learned that if I look hard enough, I will find what it takes. I also learned that although these things can be my greatest strengths, they can also be my greatest downfalls. But most importantly, I learned my words are not only important but necessary if I want to live a life of meaning, connection, and *Oneness*.

Sept. 9/09

Love is joyful as well as tearful.

In all the things I've ever experienced, the hardest I've ever done is to take care of my mom before she died.

In all the things I've ever experienced, the most rewarding thing I've ever done is to take care of my mom before she died.

Dear One:

I asked Spirit to take my mom so she would no longer suffer. Spirit did. And for that I'm grateful.

I asked Spirit to give her back, and Spirit gave me my words to bring her home to me. And for that I'm grateful.

Someone said, "Death ends a life but it doesn't end a relationship which struggles on in a survivor's mind towards some resolution which it may never find."

Sometimes we do find resolution, sometimes we find even more.

I found myself, my voice and the Oneness I was searching for. I rest with the knowledge that in the end, "We Are One."

Lou

Chapter 50

From Broken to *Oneness*

Take away my story and you take away my opportunity to speak truth, you take away the foundation I stand on and you take away all that I was, all that I am and all that I can ever be.

I've been broken many times over, enough to feel like Humpty Dumpty. It wasn't all the king's horses and all the king's men who put me back together again. It was I.

No one but me could pick up the fragments and start to piece them together. No one but me could find which piece went where because no one but me had the blueprint.

I was broken when I saw my dad crawl around on the floor. I was broken when misguided hands tampered with my infant body. I was broken when my grade one teacher took my innocence away. I was broken when I saw my mom puke on the side of the road because she had too much to drink, and in my little six-year old mind, I thought that from then on, I was on my own.

I was broken when I discovered my first husband cheating on me with a teenage girl. I was broken when I could barely make enough money to feed my kids a decent meal, and I had to leave them in the hands of babysitters as I made my way to a minimum-wage job.

I was broken when I found myself screaming at my four-year old because I was at my wit's end one day. I was broken when ten years later a doctor guided me into the "quiet room" to tell me my son was brain-dead and they wanted to know if I would donate his organs. I was broken when the doors to the surgery room closed, and my daughter was on the other side to undergo two five-hour heart surgeries, and I had to wait out in the hallway.

I was broken when I decided to walk away from my twenty-three year marriage with my second husband, and I met with my three daughters each in turn to tell them I was leaving their father and life as they knew it was coming to an end.

I was broken by my mom's lack of words. I was broken by deaths that claimed lives that were dear to me. I was broken by dreams lost, harsh judgments, mistakes I made and long detours down the wrong highways.

I was broken by all of this and more, but it was in this brokenness that I found myself. It was in this brokenness that I dug in my heels and took another step forward. And another.

It was in the midst of fear that I found strength to breathe, in the middle of chaos I learned how to find peace, in the aloneness I found a connection with my truth and in the pain I found the gift of openness, honesty and integrity. It is in this brokenness I found my voice and came to know the true me.

FINDING VOICE

Etched within
my woman self,
residues
of a child
once silenced
like a fetus
stripped of womb
causing
fear and doubt
to cast shadows
on my path
of becoming
who I am
meant to be
today.
Watching the sunrise
allows my spirit
to lift high
Essence stirs within,
searching to come forth
from the depths
of my being
Expression from the heart
seeking connection
with Voice,
a natural flow
aspiring to emerge,
urging
never ceasing.
Dreams and visions

take form
in the outer world,
bringing synchronicity
to an inner world
so I can dance
in union

My vision as a five-year-old will have been realized if through the sharing of my story you have found yourself somewhere in my words.

Since I've written my story, many have questioned the possibility of a five-year-old having a vision. My answer to this is, "Yes, absolutely! This is why my website has the subtitle *"Discover the Power of Possibility."*

I've lived the power of possibility.

The vision of the five-year-old of the possibility of living *Oneness* is what carried me forward and propelled me through life, and for that, I am grateful.

Little did I know or understand as a child that this *Vision of Oneness* amongst people, this thirst for truth and the need to find my voice would follow me throughout my life. It would challenge, frustrate, support and anger me. The need to live this became the nemesis as well as the glue that held my life together. Vision, truth and voice shaped my life and my story. And perhaps through my story, you, the reader, and I, the writer, have become *One*. If so, don't hesitate to drop me a line and let me know.

Email: annette@innerpathways.ca

About the Author

Annette Erickson is a freelance writer, poet who belongs to the online Life Writer's Forum group and for many years hosted The Write Haven online writing group. She has won an essay contest for *The Writer's Room Magazine* and also placed fifth for Soul-making literary competition and has published numerous articles in her local newspaper.

In her memoir, she pursues a relentless need to follow a vision, live her truth, and embrace a sense of *Oneness* in her life; Annette brings the reader along on her journey through life's challenges and rewards. Through her story and her words, she invites you to connect to your story and your words.

Annette lives in the Peace Region of Northern Alberta with her *female* partner of sixteen years. Together they have eight children and many grandchildren who continue to play an important part in their lives.

Acknowledgements

We don't exist in a vacuum and a book is not born of and by itself. It's a manifestation of those who have entered and touched our lives as we've walked our path. With deepest gratitude and love to all those who have walked ahead of me and led the way, those who have walked alongside of me and held my hand, and those who have followed me down my own path in order to learn more about their own.

My parents were two of my greatest teachers who walked before me. They brought me into this world therefore making my journey possible. Thank you also to my brother Richard and my two sisters, Danielle and Lucie who formed part of my journey, and have been part of my learning platform.

My son, Kevin, and my three daughters, Karen, Jody and Brenda, who I love and who have always shown appreciation and pride for who I am, have also been my greatest teachers in life.

Emily for having the patience to follow me on my healing journey and for never giving up on me even when I wanted to give up on myself.

The friends who entered my life and chose to stay a while to be part of my journey and who helped reflect back to me who I am.

The authors of the many books I've read and learned so much from on my journey.

Clients and workshop participants who I have learned from, and continue to learn from. Thank you for keeping me on my toes and on my healing path.

Bonnie Watts, for the spiritual visionary she is and for her encouraging words that have helped guide me to bring my book from heart to form.

Barbara Burtchett, my dearest friend and writing buddy through the latter part of my life who inspired me in more ways than she will ever know and who regretfully left this world before my book was completed.

My gratitude goes to my editor Rusti Lehay, for understanding the story behind the stories of my life, for her keen eye and awesome editing skills while remaining respectful and true to my voice.

I also want to acknowledge Taysha for her most welcome and very much needed expertise in helping me get my book into the digital and print world, which made it possible for me to share my story with you.

And most of all Andree, the greatest believer in who I am and the work I do, for her patience, and for her understanding of my desperate need to write. She has always been and continues to be there to support, encourage, stand by me, and lift my spirits through the rough times.

My most profound gratitude to all of you and to Spirit which I've come to name as *One*.

Manufactured by Amazon.ca
Bolton, ON

38558546R00240